CAROLYN 101

Business Lessons from
The Apprentice's
Straight Shooter

CAROLYN KEPCHER

WITH STEPHEN FENICHELL

A FIRESIDE BOOK

NEW YORK   LONDON   TORONTO   SYDNEY

FIRESIDE
Rockefeller Center
1230 Avenue of the Americas
New York, NY 10020

This Fireside Edition 2005

FIRESIDE and colophon are registered trademarks
of Simon & Schuster, Inc.

Several of the names and identifying characteristics of individuals in this
book have been changed.

Designed by Jaime Putorti

For information about special discounts for bulk purchases,
please contact Simon & Schuster Special Sales at
1-800-456-6798 or business@simonandschuster.com.

Manufactured in the United States of America

10 9 8 7 6 5 4 3 2 1

Library of Congress Cataloging-in-Publication Data

Kepcher, Carolyn.
   Carolyn 101 : business lessons from the Apprentice's straight shooter /
Carolyn Kepcher with Stephen Fenichell.
      p. cm.
   1. Women executives—United States—Case studies. 2. Industrial
management—United States—Case studies. 3. Success in business—
United States—Case studies. I. Fenichell, Stephen. II. Title.
HD6095.K444 2004
658.4'09—dc22

                                           2004058354

ISBN-13: 978-0-7432-7022-9
ISBN-10:   0-7432-7022-3
ISBN-13: 978-0-7432-7034-2 (Pbk)
ISBN-10:   0-7432-7034-7 (Pbk)

For my husband, George,

To the public I may be known just as "Carolyn," but my true happiness comes from being "Mrs. Kepcher."

For my little angels, Connor and Cassidy,

Being your mother is far and away the most wonderfully rewarding position I have ever held.

Contents

Foreword

by Donald Trump

In the opening scene of *The Apprentice*'s first episode, I introduced a young woman seated to my left in the boardroom to the eighteen candidates and to the millions of viewers watching from home.

"This is Carolyn Kepcher, the COO of one of my companies. Carolyn is a killer," I added, with a twinkle in my eye. "There are many men buried in her wake."

I was smiling when I said that. But I can't claim to have been entirely kidding. In the ten years that I have known Carolyn as a valued and respected employee of The Trump Organization, she has succeeded at any number of tasks at which the male managers who preceded her failed. What conclusion am I to draw from that fact? As a man, I find it mildly embarrassing. But as her longtime employer and mentor, I find her success gratifying.

Most people think of me as a builder of buildings. But I am also a builder of people. While I take great pride in the buildings we construct and manage, I also take great pride in the people and the organization I've built up over the years. That is the point of *The Apprentice*: to show how we build people, by assigning them tasks and putting them through tests which, difficult as they are, are valuable learning experiences.

When I chose Carolyn Kepcher to be my co-judge on *The Apprentice*, I did so with total confidence. As a senior manager in my organization, she has been performing the same service for ten years with distinction. She has learned to tell me precisely what I need to know, when I need to know it. She has been my eyes and ears on the scene.

I picked Carolyn, in part, for her role as co-judge, because I knew as one of the show's producers we valued a woman's perspective as a judge in an environment in which half of the candidates are women. But I would have picked her in any event because I value her opinions and insights and counsel so highly. After ten years of watching Carolyn in action—and like me, Carolyn likes action—I know her to be an exceptional judge of people. That is the one trait I prize above all else in all of my managers, and which has been the hardest lesson to teach or to learn.

A decade ago, I drove up to Westchester to take a look at a golf club. I liked the location because it was close to Manhattan. I had heard that the club had run into trouble with the town with regard to zoning issues, and with the bank holding the mortgage with regard to financial issues. The owner and the bank had been fighting like cats and dogs. In that conflict, I spotted an opportunity for resolution by acquiring the property.

During my first visit to the club, Carolyn Kepcher—at the time the director of sales and marketing of the Briar Hall

Country Club—conducted me on a tour of the facility. From the moment I met her, I was impressed by her maturity, poise, and self-confidence. When several months later I met with representatives of the bank to discuss what it might take to persuade me to purchase the property, I was impressed that the bank and the management company had asked Carolyn—then twenty-five—to handle the bulk of the presentation.

The first time I met Carolyn, I saw potential in her. The first time I saw the golf course now known as Trump National, I saw potential in the course, potential that Carolyn Kepcher has helped me capture in the succeeding years. I am proud to report that ten years later, both Carolyn and the golf course have exceeded all expectations.

Take my advice: take Carolyn's advice; learn how to realize your own potential. I can assure you that Carolyn's insights and knowledge of business and life are wide and deep. I know that because I know she couldn't have learned what she knows at a better place, or—if I may say so myself—have been taught by a better teacher.

CAROLYN 101

ONE

A Foot in the Door

To: Carolyn Kepcher [E-mail]

My friends have just been watching *The Apprentice* and when it ended I made a comment, saying that you seemed to be a real smart lady and I said I was sure that you were very aggressive in the business world, and that I'm sure that you worked for many top companies. My friend responded that he thought you were probably related or connected personally to Trump and that's how you got the job. How did you get the job? Please explain.

My personal agenda, going into the meeting, had just one item on it: Impress Donald Trump.

I had about thirteen minutes of face time at my first meeting with him in which to accomplish that task, make my pitch, and get out. After that, I knew the chips were going to fall where they may. Looking back, I don't recall that going to work for The Trump Organization was a serious consideration at that point; the prospect seemed too remote to contemplate. Still, in light of my brush with celebrity since my TV debut on *The Apprentice*, the irony hasn't been lost on me that I owe my current high public profile to the fact that ten years ago, in my mid-twenties, I was lucky enough to land a job strikingly similar to the one nearly 215,000 young Americans competed for in the spring of 2003, during the casting call for the first season of *The Apprentice*.

Since *The Apprentice* I have become "Carolyn," as in "Don't Cross Carolyn!" To my husband's distress, public opinion has seen fit to chop off my last name for simplicity's sake. Often these days I'm stopped in the street or in hotel lobbies by people who profess to know me, which in a sense, I guess they do. I have earned a reputation (justified) as a straight shooter and a tell-it-like-it-is kind of woman. That's not an act, by the way, that's who I am. But I have also earned a fearsome reputation as a starchy hanging judge, as Donald Trump's "Ice Queen," or another personal favorite, "Donald Trump's stern task-master."

Some people have even charged me with being tougher on the female contestants than on the men. In a later chapter, I intend to plead not guilty to that charge—with an explanation. But my main reason for writing this book has nothing to do with softening, straightening, or correcting my image. I'm more than happy with my reputation as a businesswoman and a professional, and even happier that we at The Trump Organization have been given an opportunity to show millions of viewers that we are not just about constructing and managing glamorous commercial buildings and exclusive residential developments, spas, and golf courses. Like every true visionary I've ever met, Donald Trump is both a talented teacher and a talented student, as I think is obvious from his conduct and character on the show. Under his tutelage, I have learned to sharpen my skills as a negotiator and a deal maker, although the negotiating and deal making I do as executive vice president and senior manager of two of The Trump Organization's premier golf properties is, I admit, on a much smaller scale and lesser plane than Mr. Trump's.

I'm writing this book mainly because a number of fans—mostly but not all of them women, mostly but by no means all of them *young* women, and mostly but by no means all of them women in business—have inundated me with mail in recent months, asking me a variety of questions about how I got to my present position, what I think of the evolving role of women in business, how to negotiate some of the simplest yet toughest aspects of getting ahead and succeeding in professional life. We'll discuss writing a winning résumé, making a successful presentation in a job interview, dealing with bosses, good and bad, employees, good and bad, and colleagues, good and bad. We'll talk about how to dress for success, how to manage a meeting, how to ask for a raise or a promotion, how to manage work and family, and how to play with the big boys (and rarely, if ever, lose).

Rather than answer all my questioners individually—although I've tried—I'm writing this book to convey in print some of the messages I've sought to communicate by both my words and my behavior on the show. My personal values, if you will, can be summed up in one sentence: Whatever you do, *always remain a lady*.

And for the guys, I think the same rule (with one word

switched) applies nearly as well: Whatever you do, *always remain a gentleman*.

I also believe in leading by example. This is why rather than merely laying out a long list of rules of conduct, I've included lessons and experiences from my own career as a way of *showing* you, as opposed to *telling* you, how best to handle oneself when confronted with the wide variety of problems, challenges, and opportunities that typically present themselves in the workplace. I believe the best way to understand career success is to look carefully at the people who've achieved it.

Being the tell-it-like-it-is type, I plan to tell it like it is. I'm not planning to hand out savvy advice on how to make money (for that, see Donald Trump's *Trump: How to Get Rich*). Forget about getting insights here on where to invest, or how to become a millionaire in five seconds, five minutes, or five years. I'm thirty-five and have been working steadily since I was twelve, with a little time out, of course, to finish high school, college, and one year of graduate school. I've been on the job ever since and have risen to a senior executive position in an organization dominated by men in an industry—the golf industry—likewise dominated by men.

I'm often surprised to find very bright and well-educated people who don't have the faintest idea of how to get ahead or move to the next level of their careers. We will be training our sights on sharpening skills such as sizing up a situation, spotting opportunities for advancement, and anticipating your next move. This book is for all of you looking to push onward and forward and upward in your careers.

In preparation for *The Apprentice*'s second season, Donald

Trump, George Ross, and I went down to 40 Wall Street—a Trump Organization property—to sit in on some of the casting and screening discussions. Now please bear in mind that 215,000 people applied to become contestants for the first season, and more than *one million* applied for the second.

On the day we went to Wall Street, it was snowing and cold. An estimated two thousand people had been standing in line since three or four in the morning, dolled up in their best business attire. I saw young women in high heels with their toes showing, half frostbitten. Once they made it into the lobby, they had to wait in another long line, before—if they got lucky—they joined the few to be plunked down at a big round table where Donald, George, and I were sitting. Once they joined us, in groups of ten, a topic would be thrown out and they would be given, at the most, ten minutes in which to respond—to show us their stuff.

I knew it was possible that the contestants facing me, confronted with stepping up to the plate and making their pitch to be cast, had flown in from some distant city or small town. Maybe they had hired a babysitter, skipped a day of work, risked losing their jobs, risked freezing to death, in the cold, all for the sake of grasping this golden ring, gaining this great opportunity, one moment of face time in which to impress us.

CAROLYN 101:

Opportunities tend to be one-time shots; if you don't take them that instant, you lose them forever.

I was shocked at how many of those contestants, who had put so much of themselves on the line to get that far, and who probably had impressive work experience and résumés, totally blew that opportunity. It's not that I wanted them to make fools of themselves, to jump up and down on the table screaming, "I'm over here! Come and get me!" But come on, at least demonstrate some smarts, show us some pizzazz, open your mouth, make sure we remember you when we leave this table. Granted, it can be tough for ten people to have a real conversation in ten minutes. But I can remember one young person (I can't even recall if it was a man or a woman) reaching over the table so that he or she deliberately blocked a rival from saying anything. And you know what? The woman being blocked out of the game didn't do a damn thing about it. Which one was worse? The rude one who shoved the rival aside, or the passive one who refused to defend herself? I'd have to say I wouldn't have hired either of them to paint my house.

Curious about this phenomenon, I asked this young woman point-blank, "What do you have to say about what just happened here?" This was at least, you'd have to admit, a germane topic of conversation. You know what? She didn't say anything. She couldn't say anything. She was just so embarrassed to be put on the spot, she choked under the pressure.

This book is for her.

To the Manor Born

"A whale-ship was my Yale College and my Harvard," wrote Herman Melville in *Moby-Dick*. In my case, managing a restaurant in Manhattan at age twenty-two was my Yale. Selling golf memberships and outings at the Briar Hall Country Club was my Harvard. Working with Donald Trump over the past eight years has been my Wharton. Shooting *The Apprentice*— and coping with the attendant hoopla and aftermath, from answering fan mail to putting in countless TV appearances—has been, let me tell you, an education in itself.

Before I fill you in on the details of my first business meeting with Donald Trump—my first great opportunity sized up and seized—I need to take you back to a few days before Christmas 1994. It was a cold, clear day in December when I steered my battered old Chevy up the long gravel driveway of the Briar Hall Country Club in Briarcliff Manor, New York. This, for those of you who don't know the area, is one of the most affluent communities in Westchester County.

I drove up beneath the bare branches of magnificent old trees to a sprawling clubhouse, which at one time must have been rather grand. But after many years of neglect and the addition of various wings and extensions, the place looked not merely as if it had seen better days but like one of those haunted mansions in a Victorian Gothic novel. Just as in one of those old horror movies, after I knocked at the heavy old door and stood there for a few minutes, stamping my feet in the cold, I gave the door a little shove. It immediately yielded with a squeak of iron hinges that would have gladdened the heart of Boris Karloff.

The interior was a decorator's nightmare. The front hall was more reminiscent of a disco in Queens circa *Saturday Night Fever* than of nineteenth-century Transylvania. The walls were covered with dark, smoky mirrors. The floor was covered with a thick gold shag carpet, from which a powerful odor of mildew rose like cheap perfume. After calling down the hall to announce my presence, I was greeted by a very friendly woman with bleached blond hair and thick makeup. "Carolyn," she said, once I'd held out my hand and introduced myself, "we've been expecting you!"

She led me through a lounge filled with broken-down furniture toward the door of a large, windowless office tucked beneath the eaves of a grand staircase leading to the second floor. The upstairs appeared dark and abandoned. John Murray, a handsome man whom I would have put in his early forties, rose from behind a big old desk, shook my hand, and waved me into a rickety seat.

Despite the strangeness of the surroundings, Mr. Murray conducted himself like the senior executive of a major hotel management company that he was—with impeccable manners, professionalism, and a gratifyingly cut-to-the-chase tone. The Briar Hall Country Club had recently gone belly-up, he explained, and been reluctantly repossessed by the bank that held the mortgage. Were I to be hired as his sales and marketing director, I would be working for the Beck Summit corporation, based in Boca Raton, Florida, not for the bank, or even for the Briar Hall Country Club. Any new owner worth his salt, he explained, could be expected to want to start all over, at which point we would most likely be out of our jobs. It was for that reason that I viewed this opportunity mainly as a way of getting my foot in the door at Beck Summit—which manages premium resort properties all over the country—as opposed to at the Briar Hall Country Club, which might not be long for this world.

For all you nongolfers out there, it's probably critical to mention at this point that golf courses are delicate creatures. They need to be cared for by capable hands or their most valuable assets—turf, greens, fairway grass—can go straight down the tubes, taking the property value with them. My mission, should I choose to accept it, would be to help John Murray and the Beck Summit management corporation arrest the club's rapidly accelerating slide so that Beck Summit could sell it for a reasonable price. My job, more specifically, would be to recruit new members while keeping the old ones happy. And to see to it that the club made money on its golf outings— a phrase, although I could loosely guess what it meant, which drew from me at that point a blank stare.

John Murray took me on a quick tour, noting that, a few days before, the place had been flooded by a burst pipe. Sheets of water had caused huge chunks of the ornate plasterwork in the grand ballroom to collapse in a sticky heap on the floor. Both the ballroom and the main kitchen attached to it had been cordoned off as a safety precaution. We were just going to have to make do, Murray brightly observed.

Needless to say, the place was a disaster area. I really don't think John Murray would have held it against me if I'd flung up my arms, fled from the building screaming, jumped into my car, driven full speed ahead out the driveway, and never looked back. But I didn't do that, and I'll tell you why. My visceral reaction to Briar Hall was a purely personal one: I thought it was full of potential.

You definitely needed imagination to envision the Briar Hall Country Club refurbished and gleaming for sale, but that fact was a critical part of recognizing that getting in on the ground floor—okay, maybe more like the subbasement—of such a situation was a prime example of an opportunity that other people might see as just a threat.

CAROLYN 101:
Seeing things not for what they are but for what they might be creates opportunities.

"We're looking for somebody smart and committed to put together golf outings, manage tournaments, and sell memberships," John Murray said, bringing me back from my reverie of jigsaws and hacksaws into the here and now, where I saw no reason not to admit that I had never sold a golf or country club membership in my life. That I knew nothing whatsoever about golf outings, much less about golf.

To which Mr. Murray gamely replied, in a response I will always appreciate, that he was less concerned about my lack of experience than he was impressed by my apparent enthusiasm for the place and its upside potential. To John Murray, it didn't matter that my experience in the golf industry was next to zilch, or that I had never played a round of golf in my life. What mattered more to him—because I made it matter—was that, at the age of twenty-two, I already had close to a decade of restaurant and country club experience under my belt. I also had a B.S. in marketing (with a minor in psychology) from Mercy College and had completed a semester of graduate-level courses in restaurant management before attaining the position I had recently left as manager of the Zephyr Grill in the prestigious Beekman Tower Hotel in midtown Manhattan.

While in college I had spent several profitable, pleasant years working part-time as a waitress in a small restaurant in town. I decided to share with John Murray my pet theory of how (and why) waitressing can be, if properly approached, a terrific training ground for a career in sales. Every time you approach a new table, you are greeting an entirely new set of customers, to whom you are obliged to sell yourself, close the deal, and move on. These people are, for an hour or two, your most important clients. Waitressing teaches presentation skills, it teaches you how to connect with people, it teaches you how to anticipate a client's desires and how to cope with chaos and fast pace and constant change, all of which inevitably and directly affects your compensation.

I told John Murray all that because he seemed genuinely interested—which was a good sign, because in a job interview you are, after all, selling the most important product there is: yourself. I then segued into my first corporate job, as the assistant manager at the Zephyr Grill, a few blocks from the United Nations. And I didn't mind sharing, in the spirit of putting my best foot forward, that when the manager's wife, who worked at the UN, had been transferred overseas less than six months after I arrived I had been promoted to manager. You could say I had been in the right place at the right time. But if I hadn't been qualified for the job, I never would have been hired, and if I hadn't done a great job, I certainly wouldn't have been kept on.

And so I convinced John Murray, with great enthusiasm and total sincerity (because, fortunately, it was all true), that managing the Zephyr had been a tremendous first opportunity for a woman just out of college. And I told him (because I saw no reason to be shy about it) that it had paid pretty well too, with excellent benefits, a salary that for a twenty-two-year-old was nothing to sneeze at in those days. Of course, by saying all that, I conveyed a not very subtle message that if he wanted to hire me, he was going to have to ante up.

CAROLYN 101:
Never be afraid to state your true worth.

So when, as I had been expecting, he asked me why I had left the Zephyr, I didn't try to hand him a load of bull. I straightforwardly admitted that I had grown bored, and that a desire for action and a change had brought me to the Briar Hall Country Club that day—that and Beck Summit's ad in *The New York Times*. The fact of the matter, as I explained, was that while the Zephyr did get busy—even crazy—during lunch hour, for the rest of the day, and especially during weekday evenings, the pace could be too slow for my taste.

John Murray informed me that he was a graduate of the Culinary Institute of America in Hyde Park, New York, one of the premier food industry training grounds in the country, if not the world. And I informed him about my extensive experience with catering and party and event planning, making sure he understood that even if I didn't grasp the finer points of golf outings, I had a pretty clear picture that managing a golf outing, not unlike managing a restaurant, entails a feeling for food, organizational and logistical detail, and strong interpersonal skills.

I must have given a good interview, because before the week was out, he offered me the job. I reported for work on a Monday morning just before Christmas, wearing a business suit. This was a decision I quickly had cause to regret, given the prevalence of dirt, damp, live stains, and gushing leaks, to name just a few reasons to make a beeline for a dry cleaner. Furthermore, all the windows had to be kept closed because the heating system was on the blink more often than not.

My little office, directly across the hall from John's, was a work in progress, except that the progress had terminated sometime during the Truman administration. Its one major benefit was that it boasted a window, opening onto an area covered by a tarp which I could only assume was a pool. My office was minimally furnished, and its bright blue plastic phone, the push-button kind, had a cord so short that I had to get down on my hands and knees to answer it. Fortunately, that didn't happen too much, because, this being the dead season, it rarely rang.

After quickly situating myself, I popped into John's office, plopped myself down on his rickety chair, and said, "Okay, talk to me about golf."

CAROLYN 101:
You're the one in charge of your learning curve.

John outlined the basic rules and procedures (and exotic lingo) of the golf course. I will admit that, when hearing a prospective member talk about reserving a "tee time" that week, I came away convinced the term was a highfalutin reference to tea!

A Brief Encounter

It was late in the day, late in the summer, about halfway through our first season when John Murray stepped into my office. "We've got a prospective buyer showing up soon," he said.

I must have looked a little downcast. This was the tail end

of another long day at Briar Hall Country Club, and I had been hoping to get home in time for dinner for once in a blue moon. Because we had escorted our fair share of prospective buyers around the course and club already, I knew that John expected me to be present.

"You're never going to believe who it is," he said, grinning like the Cheshire cat. My thoughts immediately ran to some major figure in the world of golf, someone whose name I probably had never heard, which would only make me feel more like a novice in the industry. But John, like a little kid, couldn't wait for me to guess. "It's Donald Trump," he burst out.

I laughed in his face. "No!" Then, "Really?"

"He's going to be here any minute now."

This made total sense, once I thought about it. One of the few things I knew about Donald Trump was that he was an avid golfer who also owned an estate not far from Briarcliff Manor. So John Murray and I set to work preparing for this visit—and by that I mean we sent someone out to buy a disposable camera. We didn't want to miss the opportunity to have our pictures taken with Donald Trump.

Opportunity Knocks

You can imagine what sorts of images ran through my mind at the mention of Donald Trump, because they were the very same images that would have run through yours under similar circumstances. Like every reader of the gossip pages of our major metropolitan dailies, or subscriber to *People* or *Us* magazine, I knew the broad brushstrokes. Donald Trump had grown up in Queens. He was the son of the prominent residential real estate developer Frederick Trump. As an ambitious young man from the boroughs breaking into the cutthroat Manhattan real estate market in the mid-seventies, he had made a name for himself by persuading the Penn Central Railroad, then owner of the land beneath the rundown Commodore Hotel near Grand Central Terminal, to part with the land for precisely the amount of money—$12 million—that the railroad owed the city of New York for back taxes.

He had then persuaded the city of New York to condemn the property, accept a fixed rental and a share of the profits (if there were ever any profits realized) in lieu of taxes. After that he persuaded the Hyatt Hotel Corporation to go in with him on the deal, putting up half the conversion cost while the Bowery Savings Bank put up the rest. Converting the battered old Commodore Hotel into a shimmering Grand Hyatt put Donald Trump on the map. Despite the fact that he never put his name on the hotel, it became his signature deal—the first of many to burnish the Trump name.

I knew that he had married Ivana, divorced Ivana, and recently married Marla Maples. And I knew vaguely that, in the early nineties, he and The Trump Organization had suffered major business reversals. Now, in the mid-nineties, he was enjoying a comeback that, as were many of his glorious deeds, was celebrated in his second best-selling book, *Trump: The Art of the Comeback*. Finally, I knew, just like everyone else did, that Donald Trump was a flamboyant showman, a celebrated negotiator, and a handsome man with an eye for the ladies—a modern-day Great Gatsby.

When he pulled up to the club in his customary long, black limousine and stepped out, wearing not casual golf clothes but an impeccably tailored business suit, he seemed just so much larger than life, which is to say larger than the image I had in my mind from his pictures. His physical presence, coupled with a naturally expansive personality, seemed to fill the entire driveway.

I was immediately struck by the fact that, in contrast to some faceless CEO of a major conglomerate, the man who plastered his name on just about everything he touched had come on this scouting expedition alone. He had no entourage, no advance men, no yes-men, no no-men. Contrary to expectations, he wasn't in the slightest bit bold or brassy. In fact, if I'd had to describe him to a friend, I would have defined his persona—a favorite Donald Trump term—as low-key, subdued, even self-effacing. Well, let's not go too far—Donald Trump is rarely self-effacing. But he was, if I had been limited to one word, *businesslike*.

CAROLYN 101:

When it comes to assessing people, don't always believe what you hear—form your own opinion.

I was immediately struck by the fact that, also contrary to expectation, he didn't say a whole lot. When he did speak, it wasn't just to hear himself but to ask a series of razor-sharp questions.

For starters, we gave him an abbreviated tour of the clubhouse, which had been modestly refurbished since my first horror-show visit. The ghastly golden shag rug was gone, as was the mildew stench, and the tumbledown place had been rubbed and shined to a fare-thee-well.

As we walked around, poking into all sorts of corners and out-of-the-way places, I can vividly recall Mr. Trump asking me—not John Murray—whether I thought it might be possible to salvage the old place. It was, in fact, the first thing he ever asked me.

Sensing that my response would set a tone for any future interactions, I took a moment to think about it. And as much as I felt intimidated in his presence, I spotted an opportunity. Like a rider approaching a difficult hurdle, I knew that not failing here required taking a deep breath and a risk that I might fail. "I'm not an architect," I carefully replied, "or a structural engineer. But my guess is that any serious buyer would eventually have to pull the whole clubhouse down and start over."

I noticed him listening very carefully. I could tell that he was taking notes in his mind, which is the only place Donald Trump ever takes notes. In case you're wondering how I got up the guts to make this prediction, particularly since this was not my area of expertise, I should point out that my father, Ray Cassidy, spent his entire career as the building inspector for New Rochelle, New York, so I knew a little about construction, architecture, and structural design—at least enough to back such a bold statement.

Donald Trump didn't seem fazed by this at all and followed up, sensibly, by asking both of us some more questions. These pertained mainly to the number of members, their annual dues, the state of the course, the demographics of the membership, and whether the members lived in New York City or were mainly from the immediate vicinity.

The fact that I had so many of these operational details at the tip of my tongue was thanks to the good graces of my new boss and mentor, John Murray. I certainly hadn't accepted the position knowing a thing about preparing budgets, managing a pro shop, handling accounts receivable, doing membership sales, squeezing a reasonable profit out of golf outings, or any of the other areas John had encouraged me to master during my brief tenure. It's amazing how fast and how well you can learn when you've got a mentor encouraging you who isn't the slightest bit threatened by your increasing knowledge.

CAROLYN 101:

The key to mastering any new job
is finding the right mentor.

Since I was—and still am—young and blond, I will answer the question that you are probably dying to ask: No, this notorious ladies' man was not in the slightest bit flirtatious with me. Okay, I hear you say, maybe you're just not his type. Maybe. But because I've given this matter some thought, I'd propose a different reason: I can honestly tell you, since I've gotten to know him pretty well over the years, that Donald Trump very effectively separates his business life from his personal life. Enough said.

As we took him out for a walk on the course, he vaguely alluded to the fact that he'd flown over it in his helicopter many a time. Well, why not? If you've got it, flaunt it. He continued to pepper John and me with more questions: about the potential of the operation, about the current condition of the golf course, about what I thought it would take to get it up to Trump standards, about our current employees. He asked about nearly everything one might have asked if looking to purchase the property. And I was willing to bet that every question he didn't get around to asking during that session he would bring up during future sessions.

CAROLYN 101:

Don't mistake asking questions for ignorance; asking questions often shows that you know what you're doing.

Like every successful real estate developer throughout history, Donald Trump loves nothing more than checking out a new piece of property. It was a sensation to watch him in action, knowing that the real action was taking place in his mind. He takes such a sheer, tactile pleasure in studying the lay of the land that you can see the glow in his eyes. Like any passionate collector of just about any object of lasting value, he applies a connoisseur's eye to long-term potential. I knew that he saw every one of the assets in his portfolio—from 40 Wall Street and the Empire State Building to Mar-a-Lago, Marjorie Merriweather Post's gracious former estate in Palm Beach, which he has turned into one of the finest private clubs in the world—as a trophy property. The wide open question, of course, was whether he saw his field of dreams in this diamond in the rough.

He spent an hour or so with the two of us before climbing back into his big black car and heading off down the driveway, whether to his home in Westchester or to Trump Tower, I didn't know and he didn't say. That was one of the more gripping hours of my life. It was exciting, stimulating, utterly engaging. In the presence of Donald Trump at work felt like where I belonged.

Getting to Know You

That brief encounter in the late summer of 1995 marked the beginning of a relationship which continued in much the same vein over the following few months. Maybe once or twice a week, Donald Trump would call the golf club to ask very good questions to which he needed very good answers. He made no secret of the fact that he was seriously considering preparing a bid on the property, but he needed to know a lot more to ascertain how much it was worth to him.

If they were about matters of zoning or other larger, mainly land-use issues, he would call John Murray. But if the area was operations, he made a point of placing these calls directly to me. I was impressed that Donald Trump, this busy man, had taken the time to differentiate our areas of expertise. But this was, as I later learned, an intrinsic part of the Trump management philosophy, which is that, rather than keep track of facts and figures, he likes to keep track of the people who keep track of the facts and figures. I was that person, he knew, on this property. I became his resource, his sounding board. I was the walking encyclopedia on the Briar Hall golf course, its good and its bad points. Donald Trump has approvingly quoted his father on the subject: *"Know everything you can about what you are doing."* I have to say that the son has adapted that adage to his own use: *"Know the point people who know everything about what you are doing."*

During every one of those typically on-the-fly phone calls, as often as not placed from a car, a helicopter, a jet, or the office, rarely if ever from home (perhaps I should say *homes*), I prided myself on having the facts and figures at my fingertips. And if for some reason I didn't, I would frankly let Mr. Trump know that I didn't know, but I'd do my best to find out and get back to him in a hurry. We didn't make chitchat. Idle conversation just isn't his style. He was always unfailingly polite and, at the same time, gruff and casual. I found that I enjoyed our brief conversations immensely. From the moment we met, Donald Trump and I saw eye to eye on a lot of things. We recognized each other for what we were: incessant nitpickers and detail types. He says as much in his book *Trump: How to Get Rich*, when he describes us both as "perfectionists."

That was the way it began, and that is the way it still is. If, as happens often these days, contestants on *The Apprentice* or people I meet in daily life or even on the street ask me what Donald Trump wants, I'll turn it around and tell them what he doesn't want:

- He doesn't want you to waste even a split second of his time.
- He doesn't want you to hand him a line.
- He doesn't want you to assume anything about him, because if you do, it's probably wrong.

With each one of our conversations, I was aware that we were building a professional relationship of trust. And for Donald Trump, trust is a currency worth infinitely more than mere money.

During this interim period, shortly after the conclusion of our first season, John Murray was offered and accepted an attractive position with another company. He was thrilled, and we who had become his friends as well as his colleagues were thrilled for him. But his absence left a gaping hole in the ranks.

I was repeatedly and privately reassured by the Beck Summit president and CEO, who would call occasionally to check in with me, that he and his organization were doing their best to locate a new general manager. In the meantime, I should sit tight and keep up my good work as director of sales and marketing. Given the fact that I was preparing the budgets, taking the nightly tally at the pro shop, mastering the logistics of golf operations, handling membership sales and marketing, and even overseeing some of the golf operations, I could certainly have built an excellent case for being promoted to assistant manager. But general manager? Not yet.

The Pitch

It was my good luck, coupled with my acquired expertise, that made me the natural choice to present Donald Trump with the particulars on the property. Yes, there was an element of luck involved, but the thing about luck is that it comes around only every once in a while, and when it strikes—as it did for those lucky prospective contestants who were selected to meet me, Donald Trump, and George Ross during the casting call—everything depends on what you are able to do with it. I knew this could be my big break. I felt excited, intimidated, but most of all determined to succeed.

I needed, I knew, to size up this situation accurately. If I did a *really* good job pitching the place, I could imagine one of two outcomes, both positive:

1. I would be promoted by Beck Summit to a more senior management or executive position at one of their other properties.
2. I would be retained by the new owners in my present position.

You won't be surprised to find out that I vastly preferred Option 2. To be asked to stay on at Briar Hall, even without a promotion, would be to work for Donald Trump and The Trump Organization. The pitch I was making was to secure the future not just of the Briar Hall Country Club but also of myself.

If that meeting had taken place today, I would have put together a PowerPoint presentation. But we went with a plain, printed presentation deck, copies of which I passed out to all the participants. I didn't even bother with an easel, or charts and graphs, because knowing what I knew about Donald Trump, I had a strong feeling that he would want me to cut to the chase.

CAROLYN 101:

The key to a good presentation is to keep from getting caught up in the bells and whistles and cut to the chase.

I spent nearly all the next week (which was all the time I had) doing my homework. The core of my presentation was a discussion of three pro formas. These are long-range scenarios that a prospective buyer might use in preparing a bid on the property. I knew that covering all the bases would be critical, so I made a point of marshaling my facts—from the average number of members who belonged to private golf and country clubs in Westchester to their average annual dues and the average number of rounds that might be played in a given season—under three different forms of operation: public, semiprivate, and private. I made a special point of doing the math. If, for example, a public course in the county might expect to host sixty thousand rounds in a season, I would take the average price paid by the public players for those rounds and come up with a revenue figure for the season. Determined not to be caught tongue-tied by Donald Trump or Allen Weisselberg, The Trump Organization's sharp-eyed chief financial officer, I took the average fee rate and broke it down by month and by season, because as every golf manager knows, you're not going to get as many players in April or May as you will in July or August. I also made sure to keep close track of the methods I used to derive these figures, so that if somebody (for example, Donald Trump) asked me, I'd be able to say where I got them.

Is there a lesson to be learned from all this?

CAROLYN 101:

Details are for backup, not for delving into.
Demonstrating an ability to summarize those facts and
figures into actionable scenarios is what's important.

If I was going to succeed at this task, I was going to have to get inside Donald Trump's head and figure out what he wanted out of the property. I knew that for Mr. Trump to buy this property, he would have to be convinced he could make money on it. My area of expertise had become operations; the three scenarios I presented were all operationally focused. It's important to keep in mind that while Mr. Trump was then constructing his first golf course—the future Trump International—near his Mar-a-Lago estate in Palm Beach, he was not yet the major figure in the golf industry that he was destined to become. He was still in the early stage of his own learning curve regarding how to make money by owning a golf property.

Selling Myself

When the morning of the meeting came, we gathered in the lobby of Trump Tower. We were all a little nervous, even the more experienced gentlemen, who despite their wealth of experience were kind of intimidated to be meeting with Donald Trump. The lavish decor of the offices of The Trump Organization is all, of course, part of the show.

If you want to do business with Donald Trump on his home turf, you step up to a set of elevators off to the side of the tall, rose-colored marble atrium of Trump Tower. An elevator man whisks you up to the executive offices and into a reception area that commands a sweeping view of Central Park and the Manhattan skyline, making the room seem three times its actual size.

I can distinctly recall being disappointed that it wasn't a clearer day. In fact, it was raining, and the sky over the park was a dull gray. Still, as our little group of mildly anxious middle-aged men and one somewhat more nervous young woman cooled our heels, I derived a certain degree of comfort from the fact that I was not going into that lion's lair alone. I felt a little nostalgic that John Murray couldn't be there, but I also felt supported by my colleagues at Beck Summit.

Technically, the bank, as the property owner, was the lead party and should have been running the meeting. The Trump Organization, as the prospective buyer, should have been cast in the lesser role of throwing out questions in response to the bank's lead. But when you're dealing with Donald Trump, technicalities have a way of being tossed aside. Donald Trump, being Donald Trump, was going to run that meeting whether we liked it or not. As it unfolded, it really didn't matter, because we all so thoroughly enjoyed the show. I know I learned a lot!

About twenty minutes went by before Mr. Trump's personal assistant opened the door to the reception area and announced, "Mr. Trump will see you now." One thing I knew was that I would stand out, with my blond hair and long legs, in that sea of suits. The question became: Was that a tactical advantage or a liability? Well, that question was answered right away as all the men instinctively parted like the Red Sea and gestured me gallantly through the doorway. This gave me a head start, and believe me, I took it.

Donald Trump's office, like the man, is larger than life. It's a suite fit for a king. That desk of his, for example, seemed at least as large as a boardroom conference table. My immediate sensation was of a room composed of windows. The general effect was of air, space, power, and light, with Central Park as the backdrop. A few seconds later I noticed that only two of the walls are made of glass. The other two are plaster and are covered with pictures of Mr. Trump and his accomplishments. Behind him I saw an enormous collection of trophies and sports paraphernalia, including hockey sticks that once belonged to champion players, Shaquille O'Neal's gigantic basketball shoe, some heavyweight championship belts, boxing gloves in glass cases, signed footballs, and yard after yard of bronze, gold, silver, and brass plaques and trophies, as well as certificates in frames, all honoring him for service to society, to humanity, or for philanthropy.

None of this stuff ever gets read, of course. There's not enough time. I kept my mind on the meeting as Donald Trump invited us to sit down. There were three chairs in front of that big desk. Off to the side was a small table surrounded by chairs. I didn't want to sit there, out of the action, or wait to be asked to sit there.

Visitors to Donald Trump's office, I later learned, typically pull up those chairs to where they want to sit, in front of his desk. But without thinking too much about it, I made a beeline for one of the chairs already in front of the desk, the one on the far right. I sat down while everyone else was still scrambling to take a position. I superstitiously believe that if I hadn't sat in that chair that day, I wouldn't be where I am today.

At every meeting I've attended in that office since, I've made a point of sitting in that chair. And, perhaps more important, the fact that I succeeded immediately in carving out a space for myself in Mr. Trump's magic kingdom means that he always knows where to find me. No matter how many people are attending those meetings (and sometimes there are quite a few) or what kinds of meetings they are, no one has ever made an attempt to get to that chair before I do. It seems to be understood that it's my space.

CAROLYN 101:

Be intuitively aware of the importance of turf possession in every professional proceeding.

Soon after I took my power seat, I was asked to plunge into my presentation. For each option, I had prepared a five-year forecast. I offered my three scenarios:

1. Operating the club and the course as a public facility.
2. Operating as a private facility.
3. Operating as a semiprivate facility, which would admit the public, at a steep fee, as well as accept memberships.

For each scenario, I explained the percentages, described what full capacity was, and made sure to be very concise. I spoke authoritatively about cart fees and greens fees and the profits to be derived from golf outings and the food and beverage service. I spoke knowledgeably about food costs, and how many meals we could expect to sell in the dining room at a particular average price.

I must have spent fifteen minutes tops. After I had stopped

speaking, there was a long silence. Were they wowed? I didn't have the faintest idea. All I knew for sure was that they could not have said I wasn't thorough.

Donald Trump broke the silence. "Well, Carolyn, what do *you* think about these options?"

I was stunned that he had asked. I was also a little taken aback—as I have a feeling everyone else was—that he had addressed me so familiarly, as if we went way back, which in some sense we did. I spent a couple of seconds, no more, thinking about that question. In all of my preparation, I frankly had not anticipated that he would ask me to deliver a personal opinion. But let's just say that in that split second I spotted another opportunity to show him my stuff.

"Well, it appears to me that the greatest profits in the short term would be if you were to operate the property as a public course. But, frankly, I don't think that public, or even semi-private, works for you. You may have a profit center, but I'm stressing only in the short term. We've already proven this ourselves by doing sixty thousand rounds of golf last season. But that's not what you're about. It doesn't fit the Trump image. It doesn't fit in the Trump world. So you're going to go for a high-end golf club, and you're going to go private. And I think that, over the long haul, you're going to make more money taking the high road."

He looked at me, clearly thinking about all I had said. Then, like the skilled negotiator he is, he said nothing more.

The Waiting Is the Hardest Part

After a brief period during which we served under an interim manager, Beck Summit brought in a new general manager for Briar Hall. Bob Thomas was a perfectly amiable, presentable, dark-haired, skinny young guy with no previous golf experience but with some hotel and restaurant management experience. I think about the best thing you could say about him was that he had gotten in way over his head.

What he seemed to like most about his new job was the title: He liked being general manager of a country club. He liked wearing the golf clothes. He liked keeping the trendy golf clubs in the costly leather golf bag in his office. And most of all, he liked making pie charts on his computer. His idea of a brilliant management innovation was to spend half a day buying a popcorn machine for the restaurant.

Probably his worst trait was his chronic indecision. He would never attack a situation in a straightforward manner. He wouldn't just say, "You do this, and you do this." It was more like "Okay, let's all work together to figure this out." Not that there is anything wrong with management by consensus. But his way of building a consensus was to endlessly defer key decisions and hope the problem would just go away.

It didn't take long for the entire staff to be up in arms. It wasn't so much that they wanted to be bossed around, but even the most capable employees need guidance, support, and direction. And since Bob Thomas refused to give it to them, they ended up coming to me for it. This, in turn, made Bob feel threatened, because I had been at the property longer than he had and I knew a heck of a lot more about how to actually run a golf club.

I was reasonably confident that this situation was temporary because both Beck Summit and the bank had become fairly sure that Donald Trump was preparing to make a bid on the property. So I did my best to bide my time and stay out of Bob's way. My greatest anxiety was that he would find some way to get rid of me before he got rid of himself by screwing up. But one day he did something that pretty much succeeded in doing himself in. It was a Saturday morning, and as he often did, Donald Trump had shown up at the club intending to play golf. He genially challenged Bob to a round, and I knew just what was going through Bob's mind. "Hey," he wanted to be able to say to his friends, "I just played golf with Donald Trump, and you know what, I didn't do so badly."

Now it's important to realize that Donald Trump is a five-handicap golfer. And in case you don't know, that's *good*. But Bob was not much of a golfer. As I watched them take off in that golf cart, I couldn't help but think, "What is this man doing?"

What he was doing, of course, was making a complete fool of himself. Now, Donald Trump couldn't have cared less whether Bob Thomas could swing a golf club. What he does care about, because he is a good judge of people, is whether they are trying to pass themselves off as something that they are not. And by trying to present himself as a better golfer than he was, Bob had committed career hara-kiri right in front of our eyes.

All through this period, which lasted only a few months, Mr.

Trump kept calling and asking questions. He knew enough not to call Bob Thomas for information about club operations, so he talked with me instead. Bob was perfectly aware of these interactions, and I tended to give him a heads-up when I was sending out information to any prospective buyer. (There had been a few other than Trump snooping around, but none of them had been serious.)

One day I walked into Bob's office and put a piece of paper on his desk.

"These are the figures I just sent to Donald Trump. He requested them this morning." Now I can't remember exactly what they were, but I think they had something to do with membership fees. They were figures that Bob and I had previously presented verbally to Donald Trump and also to other buyers. It was all perfectly routine, by the book, and aboveboard.

But Bob chose to make a federal case of it. He became enraged by the fact that he had not authorized me to provide this routine information. He was irrational and inconsistent.

What happened over the next few seconds was subject to some dispute. Let's say that I wasn't exactly fired, but I was strongly made to feel that my services were no longer welcome at the Briar Hall Country Club.

Getting Back in the Game

After I walked—stormed may be a better word—out of Bob's office, the first thing I did was pick up the phone and call Donald Trump. You may wonder why. I called Mr. Trump because

I felt fairly confident that he would be the next owner of the Briar Hall Country Club, and I wanted to work for him. I know Donald Trump valued me, and I wanted to explain what had happened before Bob got around to calling with his own spin on the situation.

I was laughing, mostly from nervous tension. In some way, I couldn't have been happier that Bob Thomas didn't want to work with me, because I had been perfectly miserable, after John Murray, to find myself working for a total lightweight.

"Okay," Mr. Trump said, after I told him the whole story. "Would you say you were fired, or did you quit?"

"I've got to admit, I'm really not sure," I replied.

"Would you call it sabotage?" he asked, meaning sabotage on Bob's part. I could tell from the casual tone of his voice that this sort of intra-office political battle was an old story to him.

"Well," I answered, "all I can say is, *you* said it, not me."

Mr. Trump laughed. That made me feel better—a little. Then the tone of the conversation abruptly changed. "Carolyn," he said tersely, "don't worry. I'm going to be closing on the property in the next few weeks at the latest. I'm going to be building some terrific residential units on the property, and I'm going to want you to sell them for me. In order to do that, you need to get your real estate license from the state of New York. You take these two weeks to get that license, and when you've got it, get back to me."

Then he hung up.

Although he hadn't come right out and said so, I felt I could safely assume that I had been hired.

TWO

The Bad Boss

To: Carolyn Kepcher [E-mail]

I know you are a busy woman so I will be brief. I just wanted to let you know that my wife and I enjoy watching you, George and Mr. Trump discuss and make decisions about the contestants and whether they have what it takes to be *The Apprentice*. I can see that you are one sharp lady. So, I have a favor to ask of you. My boss is making my life miserable for me at work and I don't know what to do, or who to turn to. At first, he seemed like a perfectly nice man but now he seems to have it in for me. Do you have any words of advice for me before I either quit or report his negative conduct to the president of the company?

Help!

Hail to the Chief

Of all the relationships you develop on the job, the one you have with your boss is by far the most important and, more often than not, either the most taxing or the most rewarding. Sometimes, with a certain kind of difficult boss—the inconsistent one, the most frustrating of all, who vacillates between being supportive and being undermining—it can be both or either, depending upon the day of the week or the phase of the moon. On the very same day that I finally went to work for the best boss of my life, Donald Trump, the irony of my situation was that I also found myself working for the worst boss of my life, Andrew Broderick.

Unless we are fortunate enough to work for ourselves—in which case we often have difficult clients, which amounts to pretty much the same thing as difficult bosses—most of us will face a difficult boss or two (let's hope not three!) at some point during our careers.

Difficult bosses come in a wide variety of colors, flavors, shapes, and sizes. Based on my own stressful experience— as well as those of friends and colleagues over the years— I've learned to break difficult bosses down according to a scheme that can help you develop useful strategies for managing their often erratic, destructive, and compulsive behavior. You may have encountered a number of these characters hovering around your own cubicle or corridor, although I hope not all of them, or at least not all of them at the same time.

1. There's the **Two-Faced Poker Player.** You've met him before. I'd met him before. In fact, he was the one who just left Briar Hall. He or she is, at bottom, weak, indecisive, and insecure. As a result, he tends to avoid open conflict and prefers to stick the knife in your back. He's virtually guaranteed to smile and agree with you about just about anything, until you walk out of his office, at which point he's likely to pick up the phone and denounce you to a colleague as a raving idiot. According to the most recent research on this subject—which is becoming a hot topic at business schools, by the way—the Two-Faced Poker Player is the most common type of bullying boss. Women are just as likely as men to fall into this category, although women are more likely to be the victims of this type of boss's abusive behavior.

2. There's the **Angry Loudmouth.** He or she rants and raves and emulates the management styles of Saddam Hussein, Stalin, or Ivan the Terrible. This type of bullying boss, unfortunately, is a dime a dozen. He is rude and inconsiderate, and unless kept on a tight leash by senior management, as terrifying as a poorly trained attack dog. The Angry Loudmouth gains his power through crude intimidation and wields that power like a blunt battle-ax. He tends not to be very skilled at self-defense, however, and like all playground bullies is at heart both a fool and a coward.

3. There's the **Snide Wisecracker.** He or she knows precisely how to reduce you, the victim, to a trembling

mass of low-self-esteem jelly with a rapier thrust right into the core of your worst weakness. In the presence of the Snide Wisecracker, you find yourself tongue-tied and inarticulate. The most carefully honed skill of this type of difficult boss is to disarm the victim with a subtle put-down. If you reproach him about the true intentions of his hostile remarks, his defense is always the same: "What? Oh, I'm so sorry! You must have misunderstood me! Didn't you realize I was only kidding?"

4. One of my personal favorites is the **Controller,** and I'm not talking about the type who conducts financial audits. This type of difficult boss conducts audits of everything around him that moves, breathes, or can fog a mirror. He or she knows where all the skeletons are buried. He makes a point of keeping tabs on everyone through a network of toadying spies and cronies. He forms alliances easily with those he can manipulate to do his bidding. But if you prove resistant to his wiles, he will make your life miserable. The Controller is the most dangerous of all difficult bosses because his greatest skill is cutting you off from any ally who might be able to help you resist him, even from your ultimate superior, to whom he is terrified you might report him. In situations where the ultimate boss is likely to be reasonable, the Controller is at a distinct disadvantage. He loves playing favorites, currying favor with his superiors, and figuring out all sorts of clever schemes to make you fall flat on your face, if possible spectacularly.

While this typology can be a useful guide to difficult bosses, in my experience difficult bosses frequently mix and match their abusive styles according to opportunity and situation. I've learned that the presence of a toxic boss can not only spread fear and terror but so thoroughly demoralize work groups that he or she can practically shut off all function.

Even at Briar Hall, and during the previous six months, I'd dealt with one form of difficult boss: the Two-Faced Poker Player, the indecisive, weak, nonconfrontational type. True to form, Bob Thomas had driven our staff to distraction because he had refused to face up to the fact that just about every situation on earth involving people will involve conflict and that, as a consequence, good conflict resolution is a prerequisite for an effective leader. Bob had avoided conflict like the plague, and he paid a high price for his stubborn denial of the undeniable. As a result, while he focused on painting a room or buying that new popcorn machine for the restaurant, the staff, who should have been looking to him for guidance and direction, began coming to me, which made him feel even more threatened, and made an already difficult situation even more tense and stultifying.

CAROLYN 101:

You need a strong sense of self to manage a weak boss.

Good Boss/Bad Boss

Donald Trump—a famously good boss, whose best employees tend to stay loyal to him for decades, unless they betray him and The Trump Organization—closed on Briar Hall in November 1996. He paid roughly $8 million for the property, which turned out—surprise, surprise!—to be a terrific deal for The Trump Organization. He had made good on his promise and brought me along. I had recently turned twenty-five. I was now working in a position of serious responsibility for The Trump Organization. As you can no doubt imagine, I couldn't have been more pleased with this opportunity—it felt as if I had just won the lottery.

When I returned to the club and pulled into the same space I'd parked in every day for two and a half years (with the unhappy exception of the previous three weeks), I was greeted by a small welcoming committee drawn from the skeleton staff who had stuck around for the off-season. After accepting sincere congratulations from all of them, I headed straight for my old office, hoping that everything would look the same. But, standing in the hallway, I could see a freshly painted name on the door of the general manager's office, on which I knocked softly.

In response to a bass-toned "Come in," I tentatively opened the door. The newly appointed general manager of the Briar Hall Country Club stood up to greet me. He was a square-shouldered, square-jawed man, tall and thin, who looked to be in his early fifties. He wore a well-tailored, close-fitting dark suit and sported an expensive haircut. In a thick British accent he introduced himself, and I half-expected him to bow from the waist and kiss my hand. I immediately recognized the type: a proper, polished, British gentleman of the old school. Andrew Broderick made a terrific first impression: he seemed self-confident, engaged, well organized, and enthusiastic.

The gist of our first conversation was that it would be our honor and our privilege to bring the tatty old Briar Hall Country Club up to the most exacting Trump standard. For an indeterminate period of time, he stressed, we would be operating the place as the Briar Hall Country Club while paving the way for the all-new five-star Trump National Golf Club to be constructed on the same site. From the way he said this, I could tell he found it a bit beneath him to be known as the general manager of the pokey old Briar Hall Country Club and obviously preferred to be regarded as the general manager of Trump National. Unfortunately, none of us knew when that transformation was slated to begin, as a number of complicated zoning and regulatory issues still needed to be resolved. But Andrew let it be known, in no uncertain terms, that he had been associated with some pretty prestigious golf clubs, and Briar Hall was not on a par with his old haunts.

Taking an Accurate Measure of Your Boss

So what did I know about my new boss after leaving his office that day? Even more pertinently, what did I know about my new boss that would help *me* help *him* achieve his goals, so that we could both benefit from our joint success? I knew, for one thing, that we were both new recruits to The Trump Organization, and that he had only about two months up on me, so we knew approximately the same amount about the company and the people in it. I knew that neither of us had gone through any formal intake procedure or new employee orientation, because The Trump Organization is deliberately kept loosely structured, according to its founder's desire to minimize bureaucracy and decentralize its business units. The construction projects, the residential and commercial real estate management divisions, the golf courses and resorts, including casinos, clubs, and hotels, all operate with a high degree of administrative autonomy. Donald Trump delegates freely, but if one of his managers makes too many mistakes, it's the street, not the suite.

It felt safe to assume that both of us had joined The Trump Organization because we were eager to be associated with the very best, in every conceivable style, shape, and form. But as with any other assumption, it was important to analyze this one for possible pitfalls. Although we were both employees of Donald Trump's, as Broderick's subordinate, I needed to demonstrate to him that I intended to support him fully in achieving his goals. But the obvious corollary would be that he would, in a reasonable exchange, support me in achieving mine.

CAROLYN 101:

When you join any new organization, it pays to get an up-close, in-depth reading of your immediate superior. It is also important to give your new boss a nice, clear heads-up on your goals, motivations, skills, and plans.

Ideally, the manager's goals, the employee's goals, and the organization's goals should be identical and inseparable. But in the real world of egos, tempers, and divergent opinions, the actual goals of individuals and the idealized goals of groups tend all too often to diverge wildly. For example, what does it mean when we say, in a professional situation, that "he or she is in it only for himself or herself"?

We typically mean that this person, for whatever reason, simply refuses to accept the fact that his or her goals can be fused with those of colleagues and those of the organization as a whole. The interesting thing about all the bad bosses I've known is that they seem to share the same delusion: that their goals and the goals of the organization/group/team are always divergent.

At The Trump Organization, we have a saying:

"If one of us succeeds, we all succeed. If one of us fails, we all fail."

Imagine an army in which every soldier's goals are discordant with those of the leadership. What have you got? A losing battle.

From my new boss's language in that first meeting, I should

have felt confident that he regarded his own advancement as connected to my advancement. I should have felt confident that we were both committed to supporting each other to achieve this marvelous transformation from old Briar Hall Country Club into sumptuous new Trump National Golf Club. But as yet I had only his word to go on. And something about his tone and style did not make me feel confident that he was the least bit interested in supporting me.

So here we were, two rank newcomers to The Trump Organization, both of whom, I could safely assume, were going to be doing their level best to internalize and interpret the justly famed "Trump style" in their own terms. From our first conversation, I received the distinct impression that the Trump style of excellence was going to be, for my new boss, mainly a matter of maintaining surfaces: of shiny doorknobs, clean napery, correct posture, stiff upper lip, and so on.

Not that that was such a bad thing. Personally, I have no problem with this approach. As in any service industry, in the resort and country club worlds, all surfaces that members, visitors, or their guests touch or see should be spic and span and polished at all times. That management discipline needs to be focused on these high-visibility areas or productivity suffers is a well-understood fact. But it is also the case that the best way to achieve this goal is to imbue everyone in the organization with a strong motivation to keep up these appearances as a matter of course, as an aspect of personal pride in their work, as opposed to the result of fear of being fired if they slip up. I have to admit, though, sometimes a little dose of reasonable fear can be a powerful motivator to keep slackers on their toes.

But the swank, smooth, and shiny surfaces with which Andrew Broderick appeared most keenly concerned (if not obsessed) seemed to be his own. Once again, in and of itself, that's not such a bad thing. In fact, if the new recruit (just as in the Marine Corps) intrinsically grasps that spit-and-polish is a reflection of the values of the group, this is a powerful motivator and a sign of healthy esprit de corps. One clue to my new boss's personality was that he was a habitual name-dropper. In my presence, he was constantly referencing the high-profile personalities from the golf world with whom, we were free to assume, he was on intimate terms and about whom he would be in a position to tell all sorts of tales, if he were not so impeccably discreet. But did that, in and of itself, make him a difficult boss?

At first, I wasn't at all sure.

The Corporate Narcissist

In Greek mythology, Narcissus is a beautiful youth who refuses all love from other people. As punishment for his indifference to love, the gods compel him to stare at his reflection in a placid pool. Because he is unable to be loved in return by his own image, he pines away and dies, turning into a showy-blossomed flower.

Not all narcissists are powerful, and not all powerful people are narcissists. But it is safe to say that among the many sorts of people who seek power in organizations, some are driven to higher positions as a way of fulfilling the demands of their egos. That, in and of itself, is not necessarily a negative. But if your boss's urge for power is mainly ego-driven, he may be one of those difficult bosses who has trouble recognizing that your success doesn't reflect badly on his own image but might actually enhance it.

During my decade with The Trump Organization, I have observed a curious variation of this psychological phenomenon. I call it "kissing the gold-lettered business card." This is a reference to the fact that on all Trump Organization business cards, the word TRUMP is embossed across the top in gold capital letters. This is the brand to which we all owe fealty, above and beyond even our personal loyalty to the man. I've seen people get so carried away by the fact that they work for Trump that they actually forget to work. Needless to say, they don't last long! I've observed a similar phenomenon when meeting employees of all high-end, top-notch organizations. Some of them fall so in love with the prestige of the organization that they view it as simply an extension of their own egos. Rather than regard themselves as being in service to the organization, they regard the organization as being in service to them. This trait is most noticeable in new recruits. Taken in moderate doses, a healthy pride in the power of a well-burnished brand can be an enormously productive motivating mechanism. But like any other drug, the gold on the business card, if imbibed in excess, can be bad not just for the body but for the soul.

The fact that Andrew Broderick had a big ego didn't pose a problem for me. In my experience, any number of great bosses—including my current one—take considerable pride in having sizable egos, which don't interfere in the slightest with their leadership qualities and possibly even enhance them. Think George Patton, Douglas MacArthur, or Robert E. Lee, to name just a few examples from military ranks. Or Jack Welch, Bill Gates, or Carly Fiorina of HP, to name a few from the business camp. No shrinking violets there.

But in my new boss's case, as opposed to those I've just mentioned, it always seemed to be more important that everything he came into contact with became an extension of *his* personality, as opposed to that of the organization. This trait played out in the way Andrew Broderick seemed to view his newly achieved management position with The Trump Organization as primarily an opportunity to inflate an already sizable ego. But he was able to position this essentially selfish trait as a way of developing the "brand."

CAROLYN 101:

**Good leadership demands a healthy ego,
but one that fuses well with the good of the group.**

"If there is a downside to being a well-known name," Donald Trump recently recalled, "it is that you become an easy target." He was referring, of course, to being an easy target for cheap shots from the media. But he has also become another type of target, a magnet for the sort of employee whose primary motivation becomes to bask in the reflected glow of the founder's celebrity image. In my opinion, if the glamour of the name and fame distracts workers from their work, they're better off elsewhere. At The Trump Organization, they tend to wash out because we prefer hard-nosed goods deliverers to craven celebrity hounds.

During my first visit to Andrew's office, I was treated to a clue to his personality. The refurbishment of the property of which he had so eloquently spoken to me was slated to begin—and, for all we knew, end—in his own office. Its walls had immediately taken on a strong resemblance to the walls of Sardi's, the celebrated theatrical restaurant in New York, where portraits of the famous actors who have dined there adorn the walls. Except that here there were expensively framed photos depicting Andrew Broderick with Jack Nicklaus, Andrew Broderick with Tiger Woods, Andrew Broderick with more golf celebrities than you could shake a stick at. In the beginning, we were impressed. In the beginning, we simply assumed that our new boss was the real deal.

CAROLYN 101:

Be the real thing, because all the highfalutin pictures in the world won't hide it if you aren't.

The Opaque Boss

What made my new boss difficult at first was not that his behavior was difficult. In fact, in the beginning, we all found him rather charming and interesting. What made him difficult was that he was so hard to read. What makes any form of inscrutability a troubling trait in a boss is that since your relationship with your boss is fundamentally about power, the exchange between you inevitably takes on the tone of a negotiation. As with every sort of negotiation, the key contributor to both participants' success is to get inside the other party's head. And the most successful negotiations, of course, are those that end up wins for both sides, made possible because both parties want their intentions to be known. The hard way to determine each other's intentions is through very strong intuition; the more cooperative way is through mutual transparency.

CAROLYN 101:
Mutual transparency creates trust.

Part of every new boss's challenge is figuring out how best to handle his own power so that he can achieve what he wants to move on to the next level without creating ill will or sowing dissension in the ranks. But good bosses—for example, John Murray—should never need to exert power openly because their power should be *implicit*, not *explicit*. Teddy Roosevelt's famous slogan "Speak softly and carry a big stick" could never be amended to "Speak loudly and swing your stick at your neighbors," much less "Shout at the top of your lungs, and when they look at you, thrust your stick in their faces."

CAROLYN 101:

**Don't wield your power unless you absolutely have to.
Power kept in reserve packs twice the punch.**

Why do most bosses opt not to use the overtly aggressive approach, even if we could? Because in most cases (although not all) and in the long run, doing so is less effective than motivation or inspiration.

Sizing Up the Power Structure

When you are entering into any new power dynamic, it's critical to make a clear assessment of your strengths and weaknesses. And when that power dynamic is an employee-boss relationship, you need to know this: If it came to a pitched battle, do you have any resources with which to attack or to defend yourself?

I decided to make a short list of my strengths, because I always prefer to emphasize the positive. I had no intention at that point of having any sort of power struggle with my boss. But I also had to follow my instincts, which invariably told me:

CAROLYN 101:

Always anticipate your next move.

Taking an inventory of strengths and weaknesses became, for me, an insurance policy. I needed to know where my vulnerable spots were in case of attack. These were the strengths I identified in myself:

1. I am smart.
2. I am honest as the day is long.
3. I am willing to work longer hours than anyone, bar none—except Mr. Trump.
4. I'm very well organized.
5. I have a memory like an elephant.
6. I keep track of money.
7. I enjoy many tasks that other people hate—preparing budgets, for example.
8. I'm young. (Use your disadvantages to your advantage!)
9. I'm a good team builder.
10. I know what I'm about. In other words, I am transparent to myself.

Your list, as well as mine, could go on and on. So what were my weaknesses?

As I saw it, my one major weakness was structural. By virtue of the hierarchy of our organization, my subservience to

Andrew Broderick was a given. He had the title, he had the rank, and I had to defer to him, within limits, if I wanted to keep my job. Fortunately, the loose way that our part of the organization was laid out meant that I enjoyed a certain amount of autonomy with respect to my two key domains, membership sales and golf outings. And it was probably safe to say that if I kept up my usual good work in those two areas, even the most difficult boss would find it hard to reproach me.

CAROLYN 101:

Know your own territory so that if you have to, you can defend it.

Getting Inside Your Boss's Head

As you can see, when attempting to assess my new boss, I had not been able to answer a critical question—is he friend or foe—with any degree of certainty. As with any other sort of negotiation, the way to do this was to try to understand his intentions. I did not yet know with any certainty his intentions toward me, but from a sense of discomfort he exuded in my presence I suspected he felt threatened by me. If he was going to be difficult, I was going to need to anticipate it now.

I soon was able to determine that he was a Controller. He handled himself differently with me than he did with others on our staff. With many of them, he played the Angry Loudmouth. He ranted and raved and beat his fists on his desk. With me, butter wouldn't have melted in his mouth; he was the Two-Faced Poker Player. He never once sought to coax me into his confidence, bribe me, threaten me, or cajole me, as he did with others. His far more sly approach was to go over my head and behind my back, attempting to isolate me from the centers of power and to create alternative power centers, to which I was to be granted no access. He proved exceptionally skilled at denying me the resources I needed to do my job effectively, but in such a subtle way that it was hard to reproach him for it. And I thought I knew why:

- He hadn't hired me.
- I owed him nothing.
- I had been personally hired by Donald Trump.

While being outwardly available, he repeatedly denied me the authority to conduct my own business, in my own department, in ways that would permit me to meet my own goals. As time went on, it became increasingly clear that he had hatched a plan to take control of the club, and it also became clear that he was creating conditions to undermine me and lower my performance so that he could justify getting rid of me.

Defense Policy

How could I keep his plan from succeeding? How could I use my insurance policy?

CAROLYN 101:

When dealing with *any* boss, difficult or not, have a good base level of performance to fall back on.

So if and when push does come to shove, you can document your achievements to a more impartial observer.

My best defense, as always, was a good offense. But my offense didn't have to be aggressive. In fact, an aggressive posture would never have succeeded, because confronting Andrew directly would have exposed me as his foe. I would have to adopt a stealth strategy, one that mimicked his approach to me.

I was compelled to become a Two-Faced Poker Player myself, but only with him, not with any of my other colleagues. To his face, I couldn't have been sweeter or more (seemingly) loyal and courteous. But while I smiled in his presence, I bided my time, keeping up my guard in this tense and tenuous relationship.

Bad Bosses Throughout Personal History

Your first boss, good or bad, is like a first boyfriend or girlfriend. No matter who or what comes after, you will always remember your first one distinctly. As with your first love, if that experience is great or turns sour—and many start out one way and end up the other—the residual taste in your mouth can have profound repercussions for the future. I was, by the time I joined The Trump Organization, keenly aware that a bad boss can, in a remarkably brief period of time, cause an entire organization's performance to suffer.

I'd first vividly witnessed the effects of bad bossing at the John Richards restaurant in downtown Dobbs Ferry, where I worked part-time as a waitress during my college years. Now you may not believe that you can learn many business lessons from the operations of a restaurant, particularly one that is not Le Cirque—but you would be shocked at the number of times I have drawn on experiences I had during my snack bar, waitress, and restaurant days for knowledge that applies just as well to the operation of a Fortune 500 corporation and the higher echelons of The Trump Organization.

For a number of years, my colleagues and I felt fortunate to be a part of a friendly, well-integrated group of seven women, nearly all of whom were about the same age. Let's just say that the atmosphere of the place was a little like *Cheers*. Whenever one of us needed a day off, we knew that somebody else would be happy to pick up our shift, in exchange for a shift off at a later date. Unlike some of the all-female teams I've witnessed in disbelief during *The Apprentice*, we supported one another without question, and there was remarkably little competition, betrayal, or bitterness among us.

One thing that was great about John Richards: We *always* made money. Although we didn't pool tips, we never competed for favored tables, customers, or shifts. We all loved the atmosphere and camaraderie so much that even after we'd moved on to further our careers, whenever we came back to Dobbs Ferry for a visit, we would take a shift just for kicks.

My experiences at John Richards remain for me a rare example of good management without overt rules, procedures, and regulations. We were a well-tuned, self-regulating system that functioned magnificently without any obvious control or input from above. Curiously enough, the only time this mechanism ever broke down, just about irreparably, was when senior management felt compelled to give us a boss.

One of the reasons our owner did this was out of the goodness of his own heart. And, of course, this is a weakness, because:

CAROLYN 101:

There is no room for emotion in business.

Sheila Johnson was the oldest member of our group, and the only one among us who considered herself a professional waitress, which may have been part of her problem. One of the main reasons the rest of us got along so well was that we were all in the same boat: We were just passing through; we treated this job as a lark and a way to make money to help further other and, to be blunt, usually higher ambitions. Sheila was different. She was a veteran of the restaurant business. And since she was coming off a difficult divorce, the owner, aware that she could use some extra money, offered her a higher salary in exchange for balancing the books, managing the shifts, and handling some minor administrative chores.

On paper at least, Sheila's promotion made perfect sense. Her many years of experience and her excellence as a waitress strongly suggested that she had the skills to rise into the ranks of management in our little organization. And our owner, to his credit, was willing to take a chance on her. So what went wrong? Sheila Johnson's promotion to manager became a classic case of the Peter Principle, a concept popularized by the best-selling book of the same name. Put most simply, the Peter Principle describes a phenomenon observable just about everywhere: Organizations, as a rule, promote employees to their highest level of competence and then, automatically, after a period of time promote them again. This process continues until employees are promoted to positions at which they become incompetent.

We've all seen the Peter Principle in action. It's a little like what happens in the third-grade school yard. No sooner had Sheila Johnson begun in her newfound position of authority than she turned into a tyrant. She couldn't wait to start talking down to people who, two weeks before, had been on her level. She became a stickler for rules and authority. And she used the slightest excuse to lord it over us. She wielded her authority as an opportunity to grab all the best tables and shifts for herself. She was the essence of a bad boss in that she was in it only for herself. And, in the end, she was incompetent and ineffective.

Under Sheila's oppressive tactics, we felt like the Bostonians must have felt when they were arbitrarily ordered to pay a tax on tea. Rather than earn our respect as a boss, or even demand it (as a bad boss), Sheila simply squandered the foundation of our respect for her as a colleague, because she valued our respect at close to zero. We had been content, if not eager, to follow her lead. But when following her lead negatively affected us financially, we began to create a plan for change, gathering late at night around the bar in a mutual-support network.

The restaurant's atmosphere, always its strong suit, quickly deteriorated. The palpable tension between boss and co-workers began affecting our performance, which made the customers unhappy, which over time meant that our compensation decreased. Fortunately, before Sheila's tyrannical and self-interested management style caused the place to go under, our bad boss moved on. But until she left it was an example of a miserable person making everyone else around her miserable too. Once Sheila left, the tension lifted, the service improved, and our tips increased—a classic case of morale's impact on performance.

What did I learn from that traumatic experience?

- That a toxic boss can wreak havoc with employee morale and customer satisfaction, which can take months, if not years, to restore.
- That one of the reasons bad bosses flourish in so many workplaces is there are so few checks and balances and negative repercussions for their negative behavior. In this case, because he felt sorry for her, the owner never stepped in to remove her from authority.

Beware the Crony Creator

So if a good boss relies on trust, a bad boss relies on (and often sows) mistrust, with both subordinates and colleagues. In the beginning, I found Andrew Broderick's managerial style baffling. But my bafflement soon turned into a mounting sense that my boss was not at all trustworthy. On the one hand, Andrew seemed to want other people to like him, or at least to be impressed by him (not exactly the same thing). He could even be generous, sometimes impulsively so. But that generosity seemed to disguise a hidden agenda.

CAROLYN 101:

In the absence of trust, even the most
generous act seems questionable.

For instance, he happened to be in the dining room one day when he overheard one of the junior staff tell a co-worker that she was a huge Jon Bon Jovi fan. "Oh, *Bon Jovi*," he said with a wave that suggested he and Bon Jovi frequently hooked up for breakfast. "I can get you tickets to his concert like this." Sure enough, by the end of the day the junior employee had tickets for two awfully good seats in her hand. I don't know how he did it. The recipient of his largesse was, needless to say, floored. And if you're thinking he was just hitting on her, I know for a fact that that wasn't the case. What he was more likely up to, I later surmised, was crony creation.

Andrew loved creating cronies. He loved having people owe him favors, be in his debt so that he could call in the chits when he needed them. It didn't matter that she was on the waitstaff and possessed no personal power of her own. What mattered was that he could put her in his pocket. He loved getting people into his corner. For all I knew, he recruited this poor, impressionable young woman into his secret network of allies. I couldn't tell, but in the end maybe that was the point: to a what-you-see-is-what-you-get type like me, this sort of secret agenda was deeply unnerving.

The problem with crony creation goes back to whether the goals of the employee merge with those of the organization. When economists criticize "crony capitalism," which gave rise to many of the corporate scandals of the 1990s, they are referring to senior managers operating their companies not for the good of the shareholders, employees, and other stakeholders but for themselves and designated buddies. Cronies are yes-men and yes-women, and they form a club within which everything is I'll scratch your back if you scratch mine. Everyone outside the club loses. Worst of all, the entire organization loses. Think of what cronies did to Enron. Think of what they did to WorldCom. Clubs are, by definition, furtive and opaque, and to be avoided inside large organizations.

The Essence of Leadership

Some viewers with long memories may recall a brief lecture I delivered in the boardroom of *The Apprentice* one day during the first season, when Sam Solovey, the project manager for that task, was forced to defend his subpar performance to George Ross, Donald Trump, and myself. "Sam," I said, cutting into his self-pitying speech a little sharply, "you've got to *earn* their respect. And if you don't earn it, you've got to *demand* it." What I didn't get the chance to say then is that a manager can only legitimately demand respect once he or she has *earned* it. But at that point you probably won't need to demand it. Respect and authority earned primarily though coercion, force, and fear tend to feel like facsimiles of the real thing.

So let's take a look at respect with regard to my increasingly difficult boss. Was Andrew earning his employees' respect or simply demanding it? On one side of the respect equation, he appeared to have paid his dues in the golf industry. He had the background, the credentials, he looked the part, he spoke the part, and if one took all those framed pictures showing him with the golf celebrities at face value, he certainly seemed to have spent some quality time playing with the big boys and the name brands. Perhaps more to the point, he had been hired by The Trump Organization in a position of responsibility. In much the same way that people should be deemed trustworthy until proven not, we owed him respect by virtue of his title and position. But despite this, he had such an attitude that it felt more like he was always demanding it.

Attitude Isn't a Requirement
if You've Got the Goods

If you're twenty-five, you've just been promoted to assistant manager, and this is your second job after college, it doesn't come off very well for you to try to act like Lee Iacocca or Jack Welch. But if you're fifty-five and you've just been promoted to the chief operating officer of a major corporation, it probably pays pretty high dividends not to get on too familiar terms with the junior staff. This thin and fuzzy line is familiar to everyone in management, no matter the rank. Personally, I would rather be respected than be liked. I think you're better off getting the respect part taken care of first and hoping for liking to come along later, strictly as a bonus.

We honestly didn't know if our boss had the goods, but we did know that he had an attitude. And what a temper! Within his first few months on the job, I observed Andrew behave offensively to staff and members on a number of occasions. I actually saw him berating one of the golf rangers (these are mainly older men and retirees who drive around the course in golf carts, keeping an eye on the pace of play; they earn a minimal salary in exchange for golf privileges) for a ridiculous etiquette infraction: walking down the hall of the clubhouse carrying a half-empty paper cup of soda. In the world of the country club, it's not really proper to do something like this, but the point is minor.

In front of a number of staff members, including me, Andrew accused this poor gentleman, probably at least a decade older than he was, of single-handedly destroying the high standards of the club. The ranger, speechless at first for being upbraided for such a minor thing—and by the GM, who is supposed to have better things to do—decided to try to lighten things up. "Oh, come on, Andrew," he said, "I promise to never do it again."

"It is completely disrespectful of you to address me by my first name!" Andrew exploded, yet again demanding respect as opposed to earning it. "It is *Mr. Broderick* to you!" To our collective astonishment, he fired the ranger on the spot.

The Bullying Boss

What most distressed me about Andrew's behavior was that it had been so unnecessary. It was certainly not a reasonable response to the problem. And by letting us see him get so emotional over nothing, he created conditions under which it would be impossible to maintain respect for him. Andrew— not the employee—had lost control of the situation. As far as I was concerned, his days as the boss of the club were, from that point on, numbered.

A few weeks later, a strikingly similar situation took place, except that this time Andrew's behavior was even more destructive, and self-destructive: He took a shot at one of the members. Just as we were kicking off our first season, a member registered a minor complaint about something. It may have been the slow pace of play, or a late tee time, but the actual issue was so insubstantial it didn't matter. What mattered was the reaction from management. I gazed out my office window as Andrew strutted out onto the putting green in his suit and tie. He let this unsuspecting member who lodged the complaint have it at the top of his lungs. I couldn't hear everything they said, but I didn't need to. I did hear, because everyone could, the manager's parting shot: *"Why?* Because I'm the *manager,* that's why!"

CAROLYN 101:

Never use your title as the sole answer to a question.

Being rude to the members was scarcely a way of burnishing the Trump brand. And, of course, this was a classic case of the inefficacy of demanding respect when you haven't earned it. At any top-flight organization, that simply isn't good enough.

Speaking of branding, this behavior—two incidents in a row—branded Andrew Broderick a bully. That label gave me fresh insight into what might well be his greatest weakness: like all bullies, he was a coward. Bullies pick on people they perceive to be weak, and people whom they can neither intimidate nor suck up to—I fit into this category—they do their best to undercut, isolate, and ignore.

CAROLYN 101:

If your boss is a bully, you're probably stronger than he is.

But who was I, little newly hired me, little twenty-five-year-old me, to say anything, or do anything, about it? This is the kind of thought (images of weakness and vulnerability) on which bullies from the playground to the boardroom thrive. My difficult boss had made it abundantly clear that he intended to run Briar Hall Country Club as his personal fiefdom. And indeed, it became clear that he was likely to get tough on anyone who dared to cross him. Though thanks to *The Apprentice*, I'm now known as someone not to be crossed, this is now, and that was then. Not that I wasn't a tough cookie back then. But I wasn't quite tough enough, or angry enough, to take on my boss toe-to-toe. Well, not yet.

The Imperial Boss

Andrew turned out to be, first and foremost, an empire builder. His primary interest in holding the job was not so much in expanding the business's portfolio or profit but in building his personal power. As soon as it was practicably possible, he began doing what all empire builders from Julius Caesar to Genghis Khan have done over the years:

- He handpicked his administrative staff. He made sure not to bring anyone up through the ranks but to bring in people from the outside, all of whom he seemed to know from way back, and all of whom seemed to owe him a favor or two.

- He attempted to deny all noncronies the resources required to do their jobs.
- He divided our place of work into two teams—FOAs (friends of Andrew) and EOAs (enemies of Andrew) and never the twain would meet.

When you are faced with the dominance of an empire builder, you really have only two effective strategies to thwart it:

1. **Passive Resistance.** Passive resistance is typically limited to grousing but also extends to minor forms of insurgency, including subtle sabotage. For example, we could go out of our way to make our abusive boss look bad in front of senior management. That strategy would let him do all the work. But the tricky part would be to sabotage him without effectively sabotaging ourselves.

2. **Active Resistance.** By using active resistance, we could have gotten together and confronted him with his behavior, made it clear we would report him to a higher authority if he didn't cease and desist. Or we could simply have reported him first and faced up to the consequences later.

As typically occurs in such oppressive situations, the disgruntled employees sought to gather around an alternative authority figure whom they perceive to be sympathetic to their cause. For a variety of reasons, including the facts that I had been at the property longer than our boss, that I remained in senior management, and that I was, to put it bluntly, a different personality type, I became that person. As confidante and sounding board for the increasingly restive employees, I had strictly limited options. I could listen sympathetically to their tales of woe but couldn't do much in any practical way to alleviate the suffering.

CAROLYN 101:

Even an insurgency demands effective leadership.

When It's Time to Blow the Whistle

I knew there would come a point, sooner or later, when Andrew's bad ways would begin to affect my own credibility and effectiveness, and perhaps even more to the point, the credibility of the organization. The way I saw it:

1. Andrew was undercutting the organization as a whole by reducing employee morale and alienating members.

2. Our annual profit figures were soon going to be tallied. I had a strong feeling that those numbers were not going to be pleasant. My own figures on member-

ship sales and golf outings were still respectable, but I had every reason to be concerned that Mr. Trump was going to be disappointed if Andrew succeeded in undermining my performance.

3. Andrew was affecting my own credibility, which I had to preserve at any cost.

So the looming question became: When does it become "the right thing" to turn in your boss to a higher authority? I should note, researchers have found that patterns of resistance to the bullying boss work only when employees can *trust* that the higher-ups will assert their authority.

Don't imagine that the thought of turning my boss in to Donald Trump didn't cross my mind, at least five or six times a week. Don't imagine that I didn't reject it, for a number of reasons, the primary one being that our otherwise ineffectual boss had been extremely effective at intimidating all of us into believing that if we dared to cross him, he'd eat us for lunch.

CAROLYN 101:

If you know the powers that be to be trustworthy, don't let any boss intimidate you into silence.

To Tell the Truth

Whenever Mr. Trump came up to the club to play golf, just about every weekend he wasn't in Florida, Andrew would elaborately choreograph the arrival, with one goal in mind: to maximize his face time with the boss while minimizing everyone else's. He was, of course, tightly controlling access to the top because that was the source of his power. And he was doing what he could to ensure that nothing untoward about him would reach the ears of our ultimate boss.

Andrew would pull together an entourage and greeting party, and a convoy of golf carts would set out from the clubhouse to chauffeur Mr. Trump around the course. Meanwhile I—who then didn't play golf, to my strategic disadvantage—was forced to look forlornly on from the sidelines as Andrew and Donald rode off in the lead cart, chatting away. I clearly didn't rate a seat in their cart. But I will say that at some point during nearly every one of those visits, Donald Trump made a point of seeking me out and asking how things were going.

Now you know me by now. When faced with any new situation, I do what I can to size it up. What were my options? What could I do to protect myself while protecting the organization as a whole? I broke my quandary down into straightforward questions.

- What is my boss's behavior doing to morale?
- What is it doing to our bottom line?

- How is it hurting the organization?
- What is it doing to my career, and to my integrity?

That, by the way, is the most important notion to keep in mind when dealing with a bad boss: You can never allow your integrity to be compromised. Without your integrity intact, you've got nothing. What really burned me up was that here was I, having been granted the opportunity of a lifetime to work with Donald Trump, being put into a position in which my success was actively jeopardized.

No matter how hard I worked, no matter how successful I might be in my individual endeavors, my boss was going to make it increasingly difficult for me, and anyone else on our staff who wasn't in his pocket, to succeed. My inescapable conclusion: My boss was failing at his job, and he was failing us and the organization.

So what was the logical outcome of such a conclusion? In the earliest stages of this realization, I wasn't sure. Much as I was tempted to say to Donald Trump something like "Well, if you want to know the truth, this place is being run like Stalag 13," for the longest time I simply assumed that it was not my place to question my boss. I chose instead to take the passive approach. Whenever Mr. Trump would ask me how things were going, I would respond in the most loaded tone of voice, "Oh, fine."

I hoped that he might pick up on my lack of enthusiasm, but I don't think he ever did. That summed up my problem with the passive approach. It didn't work.

If I was going to survive this situation with my pride and integrity intact, I was going to have to figure out some way to nullify the negative effects of Andrew's presence on my personal profit and loss statement. Luckily, my two domains had *thus far* been safe from sabotage and were still flourishing. But I couldn't be sure how long that would last. If Andrew Broderick was running the overall golf operations in the red, I had safeguarded my own operations, so that when things came to light, I would have a leg to stand on.

What really clinched the deal for me was seeing the dramatic disparity between my two bosses—Donald Trump and Andrew Broderick—and realizing that, while I deeply respected the first, I just as deeply disrespected the second. On no occasion during my first year at Briar Hall under Trump ownership was this disparity more pronounced than during our grand opening reception, when Donald Trump came to deliver an address to a large, highly selective group of prospective members.

This was the first Donald Trump pep rally I had attended, and afterward I was motivated to attend more. Mr. Trump promotes the Trump lifestyle with a fervor that would have done justice to the Reverend Ike. The intensity he brings to these messages is directly grounded in his passionate belief in himself and the Trump brand. All we had to show to flesh out his verbal picture were a few blowups of artists' renderings of the new clubhouse and course, and even they didn't matter. As the excitement died down, Mr. Trump in effect handled the closing himself. He mentioned casually that anyone who had questions should come talk to me, as director of sales and marketing. As he strode off the podium, pure pandemonium broke out. Audience members, not all of them young, were literally stepping over one another to get to me, not just to demand applications—which were not even prepared yet—but, in several cases, to hand me multihundred-thousand-dollar checks to cover initiation fees for a golf course not yet built.

That was the moment I decided that I had to do something. My choice, which even moments before had seemed so ambiguous, now stood out sharp and clear in my mind. I wanted more than anything else in the world to become part of The Trump Organization. And I wanted to grow with that organization, because I felt in my heart of hearts that it would provide me the best possible platform for my personal growth. With Andrew Broderick at the helm of this unit, that goal was in jeopardy, and I needed to blow the whistle before Broderick was exposed for the profit-losing phony he was, and I was exposed as someone too scared to speak up.

Laying It on the Line

Before working for this particular new boss, I had never had any real reason to contemplate where the fine line lies between when it's the right thing to turn in your boss and when it's not. If you'd asked me, I would probably have responded that I couldn't imagine a situation when it's appropriate to rat on your boss. But think about the issue for more than ten seconds, and some qualifications to that absolute will inevitably arise.

- What about when the viability of the whole operation, which means a number of people's livelihoods, is threatened by your boss's bad behavior and poor judgment?
- What if you saw your boss committing an act of sexual harassment?
- What if you caught your boss with his hand in the till, or committing some other sort of crime?
- What if your boss asked you to cook the books (think Enron, WorldCom, Adelphia, et cetera)?

CAROLYN 101:

It is appropriate to go above your boss's head when he or she is managing you to fail.

I also knew that there would be any number of risks involved in taking my version of Andrew's behavior to the top. Most obviously, it would be my word against his, and since he was my boss, he had the credibility advantage. What was to stop Andrew, if he sensed that I might be inclined to rat him out, from going downtown—to The Trump Organization headquarters in midtown Manhattan—first and presenting his version of events?

Then something curious struck me. Just saying the word

"downtown" to myself triggered the thought. I couldn't recall the number of times Andrew had vehemently insisted that all of us at the club should stay away from "downtown," that we should regard ourselves as a unit apart. That was cronyism in action. That's what you call a red flag.

I knew perfectly well that taking him on was a high-risk maneuver. I had every reason to believe that if we found ourselves in open conflict, Andrew would stoop at nothing to take me down, and even if he thought *he* was going down, he would probably stop at nothing to take me with him. Okay, I thought to myself, what can I do to prevent that outcome?

So many nights during that long, painful period, I'd come home and cry on my husband's shoulder. It felt like one of those last-man-left-standing contests. I wasn't about to let myself be run out of there by this self-serving, pompous bully. And I became convinced that the issue had a moral dimension. To put it in black-and-white terms, Andrew Broderick was wrong and I was right. I felt a deep commitment to the junior employees, who I knew were depending on me to save them from being brought down by our toxic boss. I had no great desire to be a hero, but there were some good people there who were being treated badly, and who were looking to me to take a stand.

I wasn't interested in being a sacrificial lamb on the altar of my morality. I needed to hit on a solution that would take my boss out before he did the same thing to me. I went to the controller, our controller, whom fortunately I'd hired, and who did not, as a result, owe his primary fealty to our esteemed GM. He was a trusted colleague and able to corroborate my version of events. I filled him in on everything that was going on, from my perspective. None of it was news to him. So the question became, What were we going to do about it?

CAROLYN 101:

When going above your boss's head to a higher boss, have a colleague go with you for moral and factual support.

I asked if he could join me in thinking clearly about the negative effect that this toxic drama must be exerting on our bottom line. For the rest of a very long evening, we put together a rock solid case that these incidents of poor management were having a negative effect on our unit's profit and loss statement. Just as I had done with the pitch meeting, I knew that it was critical in this instance to come prepared. We documented instances of bad behavior, but then correlated that with instances of financial underperformance. I personally didn't want to get saddled with Andrew's loss. Particularly if I hadn't generated it.

The time had come. We had to tell Donald Trump.

The next morning I called downtown and requested a meeting with him and Allen Weisselberg, our CFO.

Suffice it to say, we presented a pretty airtight case, and in the end they bought it. We didn't need to show them any papers. What counted is that we didn't show our emotions or just complain. We demonstrated that this was poor management leading to less than stellar numbers. My nemesis, our nemesis, along with all his cronies, was gone the next morning. Good riddance. But who was going to take his place?

As the senior staff member present, I took it upon myself to run the first post-Andrew staff meeting. It was a good meeting, if I may say so myself. I called all the department heads together and told them, bluntly, "We all know that this has been a bad situation, but things around here are going to improve, very quickly." What mattered more than the actual words was the atmosphere, which was redolent of collective relief. It felt as if we had been liberated, and just in the nick of time.

Trump Promotion

A month or so later, Donald Trump came up to the club to play a round of golf for the first time since "the incident." After playing for a few hours, he took a seat on the terrace, ordered a drink, and with a relaxed smile, gestured to me to join him at the table.

"Okay," he said, cutting as always straight to the chase. "Who are we going to get to run this place?"

Thrilled to be consulted, and having half-expected the question, I had the perfect answer up my sleeve.

"What about John Murray?" I asked in my best saleswoman's tone. "You know, he's the best manager we've ever had. I think he'd be perfect." I took a few minutes to expound on John's virtues, which are many, and his suitability for the job, which was obvious.

"You know," Mr. Trump said, "I think you're right, he is a great guy. But it might be a little odd, since he had the job before and would be coming back into such a different situation."

I'll never know to this day if he was challenging me. But let's just say that, once again, I caught on and spotted an opening wide enough to drive a limo through. Without thinking too much about it, I slammed on the gas.

"I think," I said, once again in my heartiest saleswoman's voice, "that *I* should manage this place!"

CAROLYN 101:

**When someone hands you an opportunity,
don't be afraid to take it.**

A little smile crept across Donald Trump's face. He thought about that idea for maybe half a second before leaning back in his chair, slapping his thigh, and giving a deep, throaty chuckle.

"Done!"

That was all he said until, no more than a second later, he made one remark, addressed to himself, which I must admit gave me pause.

"Just wait until downtown hears about this!"

That statement sounded a little ominous, but I knew what he meant: I was twenty-five, a woman, and had never run a golf club in my life. Moreover, the golf industry is famously dominated by men. But since Donald Trump trusted that I could handle it, I trusted myself to handle it.

THREE

The Good Manager

To: Carolyn Kepcher [E-mail]

As a senior executive of a Fortune 500 corporation, I have been watching *The Apprentice* with mounting interest. One of the topics that continues to intrigue me is the management style you ascribe to, both personally and as an executive at The Trump Organization. Can you share with one of your viewers some pointers and guidance about managing an organization that enjoys considerable autonomy within a larger organization? Any thoughts would be much welcomed in this corner office!

Survival of the Fittest

As the newly appointed general manager of the Briar Hall Country Club, soon to become Trump National Golf Club, I felt a bit like a finalist on *Survivor*. I had narrowly escaped being fired by two bad bosses in a row. I had dealt with things that would have caused any number of less determined contenders to fold. Of course, I knew that there was a very good reason for my survival. Over the past year, the most difficult of my life, I had had a guardian angel looking out for me. His name was Donald Trump.

Mr. Trump, as I've said before (and will probably say again), manages by trust. He gives his people plenty of room, enough to succeed on their own terms or fail, sometimes spectacularly. This atmosphere gives weaker players a chance to reveal their weaknesses and soft spots, as can be seen on just about every episode of *The Apprentice*. In real life, Andrew Broderick had revealed his weaknesses in all their blazing glory and had failed—spectacularly—to make the cut. Now, having survived a very tough boardroom myself as a member of his losing team, I had been given one final chance to prove myself as project manager or suffer the same fate.

Being a manager is a whole different ball game from being an employee. It involves, above all, making difficult decisions, and facing up to the consequences of those decisions in a way that can be very challenging for those who are used to having someone else handle those tasks for them, who are still learning the ropes. Yes, I had built a reservoir of goodwill with the organization by rounding up my controller and alerting the higher-ups downtown to all the strange goings-on at Briar Hall. Yes, Donald Trump thought well of me. But none of that would be worth a red cent if I failed to deliver the goods.

Still, an enormous pall of anxiety and fear had lifted. For the first time in months, I was actually looking forward to going into work. For years I had vowed that the morning I dreaded going into work would be the day I quit. But during the ordeal of the past year, I had discovered an important exception to this rule:

CAROLYN 101:

Sometimes a commitment to yourself,
to the opportunities granted to you,
and to the organization as a whole needs to
outweigh your immediate personal happiness.

Winning had taken a long time, but it made the taste of victory and the return of my personal happiness so much sweeter.

The Loose-Tight Management Style

So here I was, once again facing a potentially difficult new situation, a potentially liberating new situation, a potentially career-enhancing new situation, doing my best to see it from the most positive standpoint. I had, after all, just been promoted to general manager.

Did that mean I was home free?

Not at The Trump Organization it didn't. Our firm's management style is what you might call both tight and loose. Donald Trump is by nature a risk taker. "Every new hire is a gamble," he cheerfully points out, and he takes great pride in taking some pretty big risks on people, even people whose credentials and experience do not *necessarily* make them ideal fits for the job.

Another way of saying this is that he likes to see people stretch like one of his limos. And that these gambles are particularly gratifying when they are not, as they say, slam dunks. A current executive vice president for The Trump Organization started his career as a security guard. While he remains in charge of security for the entire company, he manages a number of major construction projects, including the reconstruction, from the steel skeleton out, of the former Delmonico Hotel on Park Avenue in New York. A former bodyguard and driver for Donald Trump is now an executive vice president of The Trump Organization and was the project manager for construction of the Trump National Golf Club. "He," Mr. Trump recently recalled, "used to drive executives, architects, and contractors up to Westchester to look at developments I was building. Now they report to him."

CAROLYN 101:

Never forget that today's mailroom clerk could be tomorrow's manager.

This laudable focus on giving employees room for growth provides us with a working (and living, breathing) definition of the good manager. A good manager is always hiring (and occasionally firing) to forge a winning team that will create opportunities for all to grow, even if some of those growth experiences may be challenging.

If we reverse that definition, we see that a bad boss focuses primary attention on maintaining himself or herself in a position of authority while keeping subordinates subservient and self-effacing. That was, in a nutshell, Andrew Broderick. Donald Trump is a good boss because he relies, above all, on trust to conduct his business affairs. He believes in the honor system, which means that if you commit a dishonor, he has every reason to hold it against you, because he has trusted you to perform. In some cases, granting this freedom to maneuver permits him to build employees up with the same mastery that he applies to the construction of his buildings. And of course, in some cases, this practice can be known by another name: *giving you enough rope to hang yourself.*

There was a second critical concept I had to grasp, which was intimately related to the first. I had been promoted, but did I really own the job? Not yet. Had I proven myself? Not yet. I was, in a manner of speaking, on probation. Part of the loose-tight management style is that you do a lot of your learning on the job—just as if you were an apprentice.

CAROLYN 101:

You might have the title, you might have the salary,
you might have the car and the perks, but you don't
have the job until you have proven yourself.

Managing Resources

A great way, I've found, to jump-start the thought process of sorting through the pros and cons of any new situation is to perform a SWOT analysis—a breakdown of strengths, weaknesses, opportunities, and threats. Make an assessment that divides up the potential factors in your path into positive and negative columns. For example, in the strengths column, the number one question should be:

What are my resources?

Your resources are the source of your strengths.

It seemed to me that I was fortunate to have quite a few resources to rely on. From spending my days and most of my nights at a golf club over the past three years, I had absorbed, largely by osmosis, some rudimentary elements of sports psychology. Believe it or not, I've been able to apply some of it to business situations. Target awareness is an athlete's ability to look at the target, internalize it, and keep it in mind as he or she throws the football, swings the golf club, swings the tennis racket, what have you.

I don't think a day goes by that I don't use target awareness in some form. So in the positives column (strengths and opportunities) it's critical to define your target as clearly and precisely as possible. Then keep that target in your mind's eye every time you take a swing. In business, of course, that's every time you make a decision.

Your target may be that end-of-the-year P and L statement. It may be your next hire.

It may be your next meeting.

It may be your next quarter.

So before you take your next swing, ask yourself the following questions:

- What do *I* need to do to get the best possible outcome from this situation?
- What can *I* do to make this situation work not just for me but for my leader and my team?

The concept of target awareness helped me put these management issues into perspective. I thought about what my two predecessors had done wrong as a way to begin thinking about what to do right. Let's stick, for the moment, with the positives (strengths and opportunities) and leave the negatives (weaknesses and threats) to the side. What, I asked myself, was the best single thing about this situation created by my promotion? The money? The title? The responsibility?

The way I looked at it, the most outstanding opportunity was the extraordinary potential, a gift signed, sealed, and delivered to me, oddly enough, by my predecessor. By having been such a bad boss, he had left me with a money-losing operation to turn around. This distressed situation, like all distressed situations, presented an incalculable opportunity for not just a win but a big win.

Thanks to Andrew's management the club was about a half million dollars in the red. I knew perfectly well that, placed against the total revenues of The Trump Organization, that was a drop in the bucket. You might call it chump change. But Donald Trump hates losing money more than just about anything else in the world. So my unique opportunity in the upcoming year would be to put the club into the black. That was my target.

As far as my other resources went, I know the one you're just dying to ask about: What about my personal relationship with Donald Trump? Having a direct line to our supreme leader was like having an ace in the hole, right? Well, maybe yes and maybe no. Yes, if I needed advice, if I needed a supportive and sympathetic soul to counsel me, I could easily pick up the phone and call the executive offices of The Trump Organization. But no, I wasn't planning to call him up every day, or even every week. If Donald Trump had wanted to manage the Briar Hall Country Club himself, he wouldn't have hired me to do the job. He needed someone capable of taking those pesky details off his desk. What you might call the Donald Trump Hotline was the one major resource I intended to keep in reserve, as my Resource of Last Resort.

As for my list of weaknesses and threats, that last opportunity pointed a finger straight at my most looming negatives. My youth, my gender, my personal relationship to the big boss could all, depending upon how they played out, be either strengths or weaknesses. My major threats were, in other words, directly related to my major strengths: Through my youth and/or inexperience, I worried that I would lack the authority, or fail to gain the authority, to instill fiscal discipline and raise employee morale. A related factor was sexism. Because I was a young woman, I worried that I would fail to gain the respect of my employees, which I absolutely needed if I hoped to motivate them to success.

Managing Perceptions

I've often said you don't manage *positions*, you manage *people*. To which I might add: You manage *perceptions*. As I entered my "probationary" period, I knew that I would have to go to some lengths to dispel any notion, no matter how off base, that Donald Trump had favored me because I was young, cute, blond, and female. I truly wasn't concerned that anyone would assume our relationship was improper. Nevertheless, I had to work twice as hard and be twice as businesslike and competent to compensate for the possibility of even a smidgen of that misperception being counted against me.

I also thought a great deal about how my image would contrast with those of my predecessors. Talk about tough acts to follow! Both men had stumbled badly by managing people badly. They also had, if possible, managed perceptions even worse. Both had conducted themselves in a variety of ways— although different ways—that had caused employees to lose respect for them. So just as it pays to get a clear idea of what success looks like, it also pays dividends to get a clear picture of what failure looks like. That's anti–target awareness.

What failure had looked like under the two previous regimes had been strikingly similar, despite pronounced differences in personal management styles. Like myself, our once-happy crew of employees had lost all interest in work, had lost all spring in their step, all the sense of fun, opportunity, and expansiveness that a great organization offers its employees at every level. Why? Because they regarded their boss—whether named Bob or named Andrew—as looking out for himself, not for them.

This glaring fact presented me with a *huge* opportunity. I don't consider management a popularity contest. As I said in the last chapter, if it comes down to being liked versus being respected, you always have to pick respect first. But one does not necessarily preclude the other. It is not only possible but desirable to gain your employees' respect without having them quake in their boots if they encounter you in the hall. My entrée into turning this situation around could be inferred from my predecessors' failure. The linchpin of my plan to reverse the current slump was to improve employee morale.

Trying on a Management Style

Okay, so you've just scored your big promotion! Maybe you buy a new car. Maybe you buy a new set of clothes. Maybe you call all your friends and head out to celebrate. And maybe you even pick up the tab. Well, I would advise you to go dutch with your friends for a while longer. Much as I don't want to be a wet blanket, my first word of advice to you, recently promoted middle manager, is not to count your chickens before they hatch. It isn't that you're likely to fail, because the chances are pretty good that the person who hired you isn't an idiot and you've got what it takes to handle the job. But what matters more than showing off your newfound status is that out of the menu of personal management styles open to you, you pick one that suits you like a suit.

How do you pick a management style? Not off the sale rack, I hope. But the good news is you probably already have a management style. It's how you think, speak, and act. Trying to cobble together an entirely new self to fit a new job title typically ends, I've learned, in disaster. Let's take, for example, the new position I found myself in after being promoted to general manager. How do you assume that authority without squandering the reservoir of goodwill you've built up with employees, colleagues, and peers?

Let's say you're twenty-five, female, and you've been working in the same place for more than two years. Well, wouldn't it seem a little bit strange if I'd shown up the next day wearing a business suit, driving a new car, skidded rudely into the driveway, slammed on the brakes, held out my keys to the attendant, and demanded that he park my car and grab my bag? What would my sales manager, who a day before had enjoyed grabbing a quick cup of coffee with me in the kitchen, have said (or thought) if I'd walked in and insisted that she fetch me my coffee?

There's a delicate balance to strike, of course, because as a manager, and particularly a new manager, you do have to be scrupulous about maintaining a sense of authority. Letting your subordinates think—for even one second—that just because people address you on a first-name basis they're free from reprimand would be a major mistake, not to mention it's an impression that's difficult to erase once it takes hold. But let's be frank. Depending upon the lay of the land, managerially speaking, you've got to move very slowly and prudently into this new transition. This is all about managing perceptions as a way of getting into managing people.

Your number one priority must be earning your employees' and colleagues' respect.

So how do you do that?

The early twentieth-century German sociologist Max Weber helped me figure it out. He made one of the first studies of the politics of bureaucracy and authority, and he discovered (or uncovered) that there are three basic types of managers, who use different methods, based on their personalities, to exert control over subordinates in organizations.

1. The **charismatic** leader exerts his or her control through force of personality. An extreme example would be a religious guru or leader, like Mahatma Gandhi or Jim Jones, although passionate politicians like Hitler or Castro also fit the bill. Donald Trump is a charismatic leader, as were John F. Kennedy and GE's Jack Welch. In all cases, the leader is an outsize personality, a combination of thinker and actor, who stirs up the emotions of subordinates and followers to succeed.

2. The **rational** leader makes an intellectual appeal to his or her subordinates' straightforward self-interest.

A typical example: "Stick with me and work hard and we'll make lots of money in the future." Or: "If you support me, I'll support you."

3. The **traditional** leader relies on his or her title and position to persuade subordinates to follow. A traditional message would be: "I'm the king, so you'd better do what I say. You *owe* me respect because I'm the leader. So there."

Nearly all effective leaders rely on a mixture of these three styles to motivate subordinates. Through sheer force of personality, through the powerful projection of an aura of glamour and success, my boss, Donald Trump, inspires us, his employees, to exert ourselves beyond the call of duty. He is a classic example of the charismatic leader. But there is also, of course, a rational side to this appeal. Many of us follow Donald Trump's lead because we intellectually understand that he can inspire a winning organization to do well, which will in turn reflect well on us, enhance our job security, and over time, increase our compensation.

But Donald Trump also exerts control by traditional means: "I'm the president of The Trump Organization. I've got the title and therefore the authority. As long as you're working for me, it's agreed that I give the orders, and you follow them. And if you're not interested in following my orders, well, there's always the street instead of the suite."

That delegation of traditional authority extends, by the way, to all of Mr. Trump's middle managers. The traditional message from the boss to the lower echelons is "You do what Carolyn Kepcher says, because I've delegated my authority to her without specific parameters."

I had certainly seen examples of how relying on one of these pillars could sow the seeds of failure. Andrew Broderick, Bob Thomas, and Sheila Johnson had all believed that they could rely on a purely traditional appeal to their staffs to bolster their newfound authority. From observing the master, Donald Trump, I realized that the most effective management style is a blend of all three types, and so I wanted that. But I also wasn't planning to reinvent myself, and I knew that I was mostly a rational leader who would have to draw out the charismatic and traditional leaders within.

For example, I'm not a naturally flamboyant personality like Donald Trump, or a guru like Tony Robbins. But there was an aspect of the charismatic personality that I could tap into: I knew how to generate an atmosphere of hyperperformance.

Taking My Management Style on a Test Drive

In the beginning, I was a hands-on manager. More so, perhaps, than was absolutely necessary, but I knew I was managing perceptions as well as personalities, and I was determined to make a point. The first thing I did after walking in the front door and accepting congratulations on my promotion from my staff (a number of whom, I've no doubt, harbored some apprehension about how I might act in my new position) was settle into my old desk in my old office. Sure, I had briefly considered moving into the general manager's office, which was a much bigger space beneath the grand staircase although, unlike my office, it lacked windows.

CAROLYN 101:

The biggest office isn't always the best.

But I decided, very deliberately, not to make that move. To do so would very likely have sent a misleading signal. I always had to keep in mind that I had grown up at this company, and that it was important not to alienate my loyal staff. I would have to move into this position of authority while remaining on familiar, even collegial terms with them. And everyone who had sat in the general manager's seat during my time at Briar Hall had left earlier than expected. It was possible to believe that the office carried some sort of curse. Or at least, that it carried some negative associations. And I had no intention of planting the perception in anyone's mind, even subliminally, that my tenure would be as short-lived as my predecessors'.

I made my first active decision later that morning, when I called a meeting of all the department heads. My next major executive decision was to throw a big party. The first thing we were going to do, I said, was have a motivational staff outing. That was an order, if a short order. I wanted them to know that I was consciously concentrating on restoring our battered morale, and that I felt we deserved to celebrate our survival.

We all pitched in to put together a big barbecue. I put on a chef's toque and brandished the tongs at the grill, aware, of course, all the while that I was risking sending the wrong signal, that I was not planning to exert any authority at all. But this is the great thing about familiarity. This was another example of the importance of turning a potential negative—they knew me as the director of sales and marketing, not general manager—into a positive—they knew me as a hard worker, whose motivation was simply to let them have a good time and blow off some steam before we all got back to hard work. I was far more concerned with letting them know that I wasn't planning to start being someone other than I was with any erosion of authority that might result from permitting myself to be on their level.

I also made a point of going through the payroll, memorizing all the names on the checks, and attaching them to faces. That included, for example, the maintenance staff and the grounds crew, none of whom had ever been addressed on a first-name basis by a manager there. As I handed out a check, I'd make sure to smile, shake the employee's hand, and address him or her by name. And you know, not only were the big smiles I achieved in response worth it on their own, but I firmly believe we got at least their value in effort returned. I wanted all the employees to know that I appreciated what they were doing, and a smile and a handshake go a long way.

CAROLYN 101:

Take the time to get to know every one of your employees.

No sooner had I returned to my office from that staff outing, however, than my management test drive turned into a management driving test. I picked up the phone to find one of the fellows from the financial affairs department downtown on the other end. "Do you happen to know," he asked, "if there are any liens on the property?"

I opened my mouth and closed it again without saying a word. Then I decided to level with him.

"I don't," I admitted. I wasn't going to start off on the wrong foot with downtown by pretending I knew anything that I didn't know. As soon as I hung up, I said to myself, Okay, here we go. Now I knew what Donald Trump had meant when he'd slapped his thigh and chuckled to himself, "Just wait until downtown hears about this!"

It was obvious that although "downtown" knew I could do a smack-up job in sales and marketing, being a general manager involved all sorts of new elements to keep track of. So what did I do? For about half a second, until I got a grip, I thought to myself that Mr. Trump may have committed a major mistake. And that the best favor I possibly could do for myself, as well as for him, would be to pick up the phone and beg downtown to find me a supervisor. But then I marched right into the old general manager's office and searched through Andrew Broderick's files until I found a folder marked "Liens."

Liens on the property? I was not familiar with this, so I asked myself: What are my resources?

CAROLYN 101:

Once you're the boss, you need to know the answers— or at least where to find them.

Where were the experts? I knew precisely where, because I'd consulted them before. Later that week I applied for membership in the Club Managers Association of America (CMAA). The staffers there knew just about everything there was to know about running clubs. And what they didn't know they knew who to ask. They had been my great secret weapon way back when I was preparing for the pitch meeting with Donald Trump that had gotten me hired in the first place. Now they would be my great resource again.

The CMAA has monthly meetings and seminars covering just about every conceivable topic of interest to the manager of a club, public or private. It also maintains a private bulletin board on its website. Armed with the right password, club managers and members can type in a question, and in from fifteen minutes to forty-eight hours get a wide range of informed and sympathetic responses. The CMAA is a support group for people who every day are faced with all sorts of problems that they can't possibly have anticipated. For example, I can go to the site and type in "A golf ball just hit a car driving by. Can someone give me a heads-up on the legal issues involved?"

By the end of the day, I'll get a slew of responses. "According to case number such-and-such" or "I've had a similar situation at my club."

My point, of course, is not to encourage *you* to join the CMAA unless you happen to be a country club manager. But it is to show you one of the ways you can seek out the optimum resources in your field to obtain the knowledge you need to function effectively.

Trying to Be All Things to All People

At one point, a month before the close of the golf season in November, we lost a chef. I had the option of hiring a rent-a-chef but instead I decided we would all take over, picking up on the "let's pitch in" tone I'd set at the staff outing. We cooked for parties of 150 people, all simple chicken entrées, barbecues, and buffets, mind you, but I was still at the grill with my staff. Now you could say that by doing all this myself, I risked losing their respect, because I would project an image that they would not consider authoritative enough. If I put myself on their level, as they say, they wouldn't be able to see me as a leader. But what I had actually done was to put all of us on pretty much the same level, as peers and partners and players.

During our chefless phase, we covered six or seven events together, and at some point nearly every member of the senior staff filled in, chopping onions, preparing sauces, whatever needed to get done. I probably wouldn't do it today because I've been promoted a few times since then, but you know what? Rather than being terrible chores, those events were a blast, not just for the members and guests but for the staff. In part because I'd been working there for more than two years, and in part because of the ordeal we'd all just been through, I got more respect from the staff more quickly by walking around in that apron and toque than I could have in any other way.

CAROLYN 101:

Showing authority can be as simple as doing what needs to get done.

This hands-on approach fit rather neatly into my two-pronged program for club improvement, which combined enhancements to employee morale with tighter fiscal management. That is, by the way, an elegant way of saying that, as a manager, I'm exceedingly cost-conscious. The only thing I love more than making money is saving money. And so I didn't stop at minding the gas grill. I also handled the money.

I did this, of course, with a specific end in mind: a profit and loss statement at the end of the year that stated a profit.

A profit you couldn't sneeze at.

A profit Donald Trump wouldn't sneeze at.

How to Make a Management Mistake and Live to Tell the Tale

During a period when we were between controllers, I committed my first major management error. One of our junior employees had left, and since in this case it was appropriate to give a severance package, I made myself responsible for putting it together. But I did a stupid thing—I made an incorrect calculation and processed paperwork for twice as much as would have been appropriate.

Fortunately for me, if not for him, I caught my error early and placed a desperate call to the financial affairs department downtown.

"Shit, Jeff, I screwed up!"

"Okay," he said calmly, after I'd explained the fiasco. "We can fix this. You stopped his direct deposit, right?"

"Jeff." My heart hit my stomach. I hadn't thought to do that. So all of that extra salary could have been sitting in this ex-employee's account, just when I'd been going to such cost-cutting lengths to turn a profit.

After I told him that I hadn't done that either, he replied, "I'll see what I can do."

I got a call a few minutes later from the CFO of The Trump Organization. He is someone I deeply admire, and therefore did not want to disappoint.

"Carolyn, what the hell happened here?"

"Allen," I said, trying to keep the emotion out of my voice, "what can I say? I screwed up."

I wasn't interested in making excuses.

CAROLYN 101:

If you make a mistake, don't make excuses and don't be afraid to ask for help.

"We're going to try to cancel the direct deposit," he said, "and we'll do what we have to do to get the excess payment back."

The rest of the day felt dark and gloomy until I got a return call from Allen.

"Carolyn," he said gently, "we've taken care of it. And by the way, people make mistakes. We're the accounting staff here. We're here for your support, so when you do make mistakes, we're here to back you up."

"Thanks, Allen," I said, after profusely apologizing, which by the way is a good thing to do after making a mistake.

CAROLYN 101:

A sincere and heartfelt apology gets you more respect than trying to wriggle out of owning up to a mistake.

Contrary to popular wisdom—and this is something I wish more politicians understood—saying you're sorry doesn't make you seem weak, it makes you seem strong.

Allen and I also discussed the possibility that trying to save a few weeks of a controller's salary might have been a rare example, in my case, of being penny wise and pound foolish. I didn't mention, because it wasn't necessary, that if I hadn't caught my error, probably no one else would have. The employee would certainly not have been inclined to say anything, and at the club I was, for better or worse, in charge of the books. So I learned an important lesson, which was that trying to cut corners isn't always the thing to do.

It was fortunate that the accounting staff was able to help me, the GM pinch-hitting as controller to catch the error in the nick of time. But there was also another management lesson to be learned here.

CAROLYN 101:

If you have created a reservoir of goodwill, with superiors
as well as subordinates, when things go awry—
as they inevitably will—you can draw on that to
help you come through unscathed.

It is also worth pointing out that our CFO's response was the essence of good management. He was not my boss, and I didn't report to him. But he recognized that his role was to support the operating units to the best of his ability.

And, speaking of reservoirs of goodwill, our particular operating unit was doing better than anticipated. I later realized that one of the reasons Allen hadn't been harder on me was he knew that not just I, but all of us at Briar Hall, had been humping to pull a profit. He had been carefully reviewing our monthly P and L statements, and he must have liked what he saw. Not long thereafter, our annual numbers came in. We had turned a profit of a little over $500,000.

I wasn't in Donald Trump's office that day, but I wish I had been. People who were present told me later that he brandished our P and L printout for all to see, announcing "There've been many men before her who have run this place, and they've all run it in the red!"

You would have thought he'd just hit the jackpot at the Taj Mahal.

Now when "downtown" wondered—maybe sometimes out loud—if he'd made the right choice in picking me, he had hard evidence to back up his choice. And I didn't mind in the slightest that he took total credit for having given me the assignment and tended—in the retelling—not to focus on the fact that I had been the one who planted the idea in his head. I've said that management at The Trump Organization is management by trust. But what I haven't said is that this philosophy is based on the fact that Donald Trump, above all, trusts himself.

FOUR

The Good Employee

To: Carolyn Kepcher [E-mail]

I just wanted to tell you that I think you are doing such a great job on *The Apprentice*. The show is great, but as I watch it with my family, I find myself always wondering what you are thinking. You seem to have such a good relationship with your superiors and I admire your dedication and work ethic. As an employee, I am constantly thinking about how to impress my boss so that I can rise to the next level. I was hoping you might be able to share with me some of the secrets of your success as an employee.

The Key

What's the premise of *The Apprentice*? May the best employee win. Through a process of Darwinian elimination, survival of the fittest, we select that person who most skillfully disposes of a series of assigned tasks, all of which require problem-solving skills, teamwork, leadership, motivation, creativity, and—last but not least—hard work. It's a multiweek marathon of a job interview, with one goal in mind: to root out the best employee, whom we can assume will make the best apprentice to Donald Trump. But what are our criteria? Not manual skills but leadership skills. Not physical dexterity but interpersonal dexterity. Not brawn but brains. At The Trump Organization, what we looking for in a good employee is a good future manager.

As managers at every level, we have as our primary responsibility to recruit, initiate, motivate, inspire, and train employees capable of one day taking our place. That is why all successful managers are at heart mentors and teachers as much as bosses. Take Donald Trump, Warren Buffett, or Bill Gates: all inspire themselves to inspire others. And as managers we are looking to you, our employees, to be ready, able, and willing to absorb the tough lessons it takes to become a successful manager and, in turn, be able to train new managers to take your place at the top.

So here's the good news: I can tell you what it takes to be a good employee in less than ten seconds. In fact, I can sum it up in one sentence:

CAROLYN 101:

A good employee is the master of his or her domain.

Let me explain. Let's say you are an assistant groundskeeper at one of our properties. Your job is to keep a section of the grounds clean and well cared for. You are the boss of that section. Everything that goes on there is your responsibility. Or let's say you are a junior accounts supervisor in an advertising agency. Your job is to own those accounts at the level of responsibility you have been assigned. You need to define an area of responsibility that is entirely yours and then make that area outstanding. That is how you get your boss's attention, and rise to the next level.

Anticipating Your Next Move

Only once you have mastered the domain you have been assigned will your superiors consider you for promotion. Mastery of your current domain is your platform. But with every promotion, your superiors' primary uncertainty is always: Is he or she ready to take this next step?

The best way to demonstrate that you are ready to assume new responsibilities is to learn about these responsibilities in advance. Every area of responsibility is a new field of knowledge, and it is possible to learn a great deal before actually practicing it. This is, after all, what it means to be an apprentice. When I was the newly hired director of sales and marketing at Briar Hall, I made a point of learning as much as I could about those areas I would need some knowledge of before becoming a general manager—bookkeeping, budgeting, permitting, maintenance. But a word of warning: Demonstrating to your superiors that you are prepared to take the next step means finding a way to learn about the areas outside your immediate domain without stepping on anyone's toes or giving the impression that you want someone else's job. At least not before you are prepared to move up by proving yourself at your current level.

CAROLYN 101:

Promoting yourself is the best way to get promoted.

Every Employee, at Every Level, Is a Salesman

I don't care what you do or how much you get paid, if you're working for me, you are going to be selling our product. So what's the product? First of all, the product is yourself. Second of all, it's our organization. Third of all—and the order is important—it's the product or service you are actually selling, whether that be a club membership, a home, or a thousand shares of stock. Nobody is going to buy our organization—or anything else we sell—from you until they have bought *you*.

Once again, as a former star waitress, I will use waiting on tables as an example. The moment you make contact with those customers, you are selling yourself. They are looking at you, gauging your credibility. If they ask whether you like the fish, they are looking for you to tell them the truth, not give them some spin. Once you've established beyond a shadow of a doubt that you're credible, you can sell them just about anything. But that is Sales 101. What I am saying here is that you have to take the Sales 101 mind-set and apply it to every new task, every new assignment, every new situation, and keep on selling yourself, your organization, and your product or service until such time as you get new tasks, projects, and assignments to tackle, and then you can start selling all over again.

Here at The Trump Organization, we take seriously the idea that the young man or woman, possibly a college kid on summer break, possibly a career service professional, who takes your bag or handles your clubs or opens the door is a salesperson of the first order for the organization as a whole, with Donald Trump being, of course, our A–Number One salesman.

Getting Hired

Put yourself in the place of the contestants on *The Apprentice*. I can't tell you how many letters and e-mails I get asking, "How can I get hired by The Trump Organization?" It isn't easy, but I will be happy to give you some tips on what I think makes a good potential hiree. Let's begin our seminar on the hiring process from the beginning.

Every new hire is a stab in the dark based on a remarkably slim body of evidence: an application, a résumé, a reference, an interview, most of which take only minutes, if not seconds, of our time. Unlike in the world of *The Apprentice*, in my office I don't have thirteen weeks in which to make up my mind about you. I will expend whole minutes—as opposed to seconds—only on candidates who, based on a good first impression and strong credentials, seem capable of making it through the first round.

How do you get me to spend more than five seconds on your application? It's so easy for me to reject you. You have to make it hard for me to reject you.

CAROLYN 101:
Getting a job is a job unto itself.

Like any other job, you have to attack this problem—your lack of a job—with verve, tenacity, and imagination. The most important thing is to think before sending out those cover letters and résumés to everyone under the sun who might hire you. You need to do your homework on the subject of yourself, then do your homework on the needs of a prospective employer. You need to make a strong, logical case not that you need us but that we need you. That is where the salesman part comes in. You need to sell me on you. Every product has a USP (unique selling proposition). What's yours?

CAROLYN 101:
Convince me that I need you.

What am I looking for in an employee? Someone to make my life simpler. As a manager operating under continual pressure to perform, I am burdened by people who make my life complicated, and this is one way you can make my job less complicated. I want someone with whom I feel comfortable delegating the decisions that I would make if I had the time. As my prospective employee, start thinking as if you are already my employee.

CAROLYN 101:

To get the job, act as if you already work here.

Once again, put yourself in my shoes. I'd like to get this process over as quickly as possible and get back to work. What would be easier for me than if you give me a great cover letter, a great résumé, a great interview, and I hire you, you do a great job, and you get promoted? Help me make this difficult decision about hiring you. Make yourself into a slam dunk.

The best way to do that is to walk into my office for the interview with self-confidence and pride, as if there is not a doubt in your mind that you can do this job. This is not about being arrogant or cocky. That sort of thing doesn't work here after you're hired, much less before. I mean you need to convey a sense of quiet competence. Show me that you are utterly prepared, if I do hire you, to walk in here and, from day one, start delivering the goods.

Résumé, Cover Letter, and Pre-interview Don'ts

1. Try to interview my secretary if you want the job. This prohibition includes:
   - Calling my secretary and asking, "Could you describe the job to me?"
   - Asking her on the phone, before coming in, "What's the pay?" (If we didn't put it in the ad, there was a *reason.*)
   - Saying to my secretary, "Well, I want to see if it's worth my time making the trip down." My response always will be: "Don't waste my time."

2. Spell my name or get my title wrong on your cover letter. Take the time to get all the details correct. If I note a misspelling on your cover letter or résumé, it goes in the garbage. If you get my title wrong, it's in the garbage. I made that mistake once myself, early on, and you know what? The only reason my résumé and cover letter didn't end up in the garbage was that they were miraculously intercepted by a friend who happened to work at the company and I was able to resend my package without anyone being the wiser. Don't count on miracles. Use the spell-checker. And confirm your facts.

3. Apply for a position for which you have zero experience. The impression I'm going to get is that you sent your résumé out indiscriminately, and that you've got

a scattershot approach to life, which I don't need in an employee.

4. Apply for a position with me when you've had five jobs in six years. If you come in with two jobs in five or six years, and one is a promotion to the other, that's more like it. If you've got a great résumé that says you recently started a new job, I don't want you either.

5. Call me repeatedly if you've sent in your résumé and cover letter and I don't call you. I committed this mistake once, and I still cringe at the thought. Just after graduating from college, before I knew better, I repeatedly called a club in Tarrytown that didn't respond to my résumé or my calls. Take my word for it: If they don't call you, calling them won't help. It's just like dating. The rules never change.

6. Start out your cover letter "I'm the person for you." Or, my personal favorite, "I know what you're looking for." Also on my blacklist are the following: "I know what Donald Trump is looking for, and I'm that person." Remember, you're interviewing with me, not Mr. Trump.

7. Send a cover letter that looks as if you've just filled in the blanks on a word-processing template. Show a little more imagination.

8. State in your cover letter, "I want this job because—" A better way to put the same thing is to stress "What *I* can do for *you.*"

Now a few résumé and cover letter do's.

Résumé, Cover Letter, and Pre-interview Do's

1. Write a *short* cover letter, even for a major position. Don't give me a four-page essay on who you are and why you want the job. Put yourself in my shoes. I'm looking for someone who knows how to be succinct, how to take a complex idea and render it into a few well-thought-out bullet points. I'm looking for someone to take some of the work off my back. So why not start now?

2. Tell me, in a few short sentences, what you've done, where you've done it, why you think that what you've done is relevant to the present position. I need you to give me the material to make a case for you. "I've been in the sales force doing marketing research for Company ABC, and I can utilize my skills to—" is a fine way to begin.

3. Show me you know my company and the job you're applying for. I want you to say specifically, "I understand you're hiring for the director of sales and marketing. I think that my experience makes me the right person for the job."

Your résumé and cover letter have passed muster! I've just called you in for a interview. Here's where the going gets tough and the tough get going.

Interview Don'ts

1. Come in looking as if you're planning to spend a day at the beach. I am a professional. So are you. *Look* the part. *Dress* the part. *Be* the part.

2. Plunk yourself down in a chair without so much as a by-your-leave. Wait for me to invite you to sit down. Don't worry, I will. And don't lean back too far in that chair and cross your legs casually as if we're friends. I don't want to hire a slouch.

3. Lead with information about your personal life, particularly if it has no bearing on your capacity to handle the job. I once interviewed a woman to be a restaurant manager who came in with a strong résumé but blew the interview in the first five seconds by saying, "I'm a recently divorced single mother of two." I didn't give a hoot if she was divorced or lived on the moon. I wasn't impressed that she started out with this particular fact—it made me wonder if she was asking me to cut her some slack. I wanted to know if she could do the job. In any interview, it's important not to lead with a fact that raises more questions than it answers.

4. Start with a question. When I hear at the beginning of an interview, "Tell me what it will take for me to succeed in this job," the alarm bell goes off. The problem with starting out with such a question is twofold:

   • It makes me feel as if *you* are trying to interview me.

- It seems lazy. I need you to be thinking about what it will take to succeed at the job.

5. Say, "Gee, that sounds exciting," if I do decide to explain the job to you. I want you to be excited before you enter my office, and bring that excitement in here.

6. Hand me a line if I ask you why you left your last job. As far as I'm concerned, if the answer is "Well" (after hemming and hawing and looking at the floor) "my manager and I didn't get along," the interview ends then and there. Your job should be to get along with your manager. If you didn't, don't tell me about it. Honesty is usually the best policy, but don't bring this matter up if I don't ask you. If I do ask, try to tell me the story in a way that unfailingly stresses the positive points of the situation and your role in it without undermining or bad-mouthing anyone else. Keep in mind that I am your prospective manager, and at your next job interview, I don't want you bad-mouthing me.

Here's an example of what *not* to do in handling these sensitive situations. When the Trump National Golf Club first opened, I needed to hire a controller. A promising candidate who had worked at a prestigious club in New York came in.

"So," I asked him, "why did you leave Brentbrook?"

"I left Brentbrook," he responded, in a voice that bristled with resentment, "because the manager there was *so* unimaginative. He didn't listen to any of my ideas. He came up with a few decent ideas, but my ideas were better. He didn't listen to me. All he wanted to do was promote *his* ideas."

Tell me what is wrong with this picture. My basic reaction to this tale of woe (although I didn't say it outright) was "Get over it. And while you're at it, get out of my office. It's really stupid to tell me how bad your senior is, and we don't hire idiots here."

Curiously enough, a few years went by and I needed to hire a controller for our newly opened Bedminster, New Jersey, property. Somehow I ended up meeting this same candidate again. I couldn't remember what it was about him that had bugged me until he opened his mouth. It was the same old story, only set at a different club, with a different narrow-minded manager.

So what do you do when you didn't get along with your last manager? As you know that I know, not every superior is a good egg. And some are rotten. But that's not really the point in this situation, is it? Think about where you are *now*. Isn't that why you're *here* and not *there*? The point is calmly, carefully, and subtly to steer our conversation toward some aspect of your work and your life where you can demonstrate a positive attitude, and tell me an anecdote in which you can impress me by having done something that benefited your previous company. Tell me why you succeeded, not why you failed.

Interview Do's

1. Call me *Ms.* Kepcher. It's a common courtesy that I appreciate. Unless we've been introduced socially, calling me by my first name is too informal.

2. Give me something I'm going to remember after you're gone. I don't mean wear a Day-Glo tie or say "Howdy!" Tell me a great story. Or better yet, tell me a great story that shows you *at your best*. You've got five minutes here, and the most important thing I am looking for is how effectively you seize opportunities and utilize your time and mine.

3. Show me your confidence level. I want you to come in selling yourself, creating credibility from the moment you enter. Show me self-confidence. Show me that you know who you are. Just be clear, crisp, calm, and professional. Remember, no matter what position we are trying to fill, I want to hire a future manager. And I want to see you upbeat and positive about being the perfect person to fill this position. If you have the slightest doubt about it, don't bother.

The Click

So what am I really looking for in an employee? I am looking most for The Click. None of these do's and don'ts can possibly compete with it. You all know what The Click is, because you've heard it yourself. It can happen when meeting a man or a woman, a colleague at work or a stranger standing in line at the airport. It's that subtle thing that happens when you connect with someone for the first time. So if I'm going to hire you, I've got to feel that click that says you'll mesh with my crew. I'll sift through five thousand résumés and conduct five hundred interviews, and if I don't hear that click, or feel that click, I'm going to keep meeting candidates until I do. What The Click tells me, in an intuitive flash, is whether the person I'm talking to stands a good chance of doing the job and fitting in with our team. That is my overriding priority in filling any position.

Let me give you an example of how The Click works, and how when it does I might even create a job for you. Not long ago I attended a PGA trade show in Florida, as I do frequently, since it is a good networking opportunity. Every night after the exhibition closes down there's a big function, with a lobby bar and hundreds of people milling around. I was standing in a group when a man came up to me and started talking. He was a head golf pro, he told me, so I asked him where he worked.

"I just left a course in Westchester County," he replied casually, "and right now I'm in between jobs." Someone had recently asked him to help with a development project for a golf course somewhere in the South. As he began describing his involvement with this project, I found his perspective on its problems compelling. And the more we spoke, the more I found *him* compelling.

Without thinking much about it, I handed him my business card.

"I think I want you to work for me," I said, "but I have no idea in what capacity. I've got a golf pro already, whom I'm incredibly happy with."

Having The Click meant everything. I barely glanced at his résumé, and my main question was how he would fit in with our group. A week or two later I called and asked him to come in for a chat. "This is not a formal job interview," I said. "I just wanted to talk some more about what you might be able to do for us around here."

I made a point of not thinking too much about where he might fit in before our conversation. I wanted the conversation, if possible, to lead us to where we wanted to go.

"I know you're a golf pro," I started out, "but I want to discuss the possibility that you might fit in here somewhere else."

We talked for a while, and it dawned on me: this man was a good or great salesman. And I knew it from the way he had, in effect, sold himself to me at the trade show without even meaning to. He and I had both immediately understood that some sort of personal connection has to precede the professional connection. Now that I had my hook, it was only a matter of time before we caught the fish—the right niche for him in our organization.

"How would you feel about getting involved in selling memberships and running tournaments?" I asked. I could sense him mentally trying this idea on for size, and not being sure it was a good fit.

"Think about it," I urged. "Don't say yes or no now, because this is going to be a major lifestyle and professional change for you if you do it."

A couple of days later he came back and said, "I'm really interested in the job."

I asked him why.

He responded that he wanted to be part of our operation. And he felt that once he had a foot in the door, it was a place he would be interested in taking root and growing.

For me The Click is the most important thing because management is about motivating good people, so you need good people to motivate. I ascribe 99.9 percent of my success as a manager to knowing how to hire good people, and to knowing that most of the hiring process is intuitive as opposed to analytical. My personal management style is all about forging a high-performance team.

Good Employee Rules

So you've made the cut. You've just been hired as my personal apprentice. Just so you know, with the territory come some rules:

GOOD EMPLOYEE RULE 1:
If one player wins, we all win; if one player loses, we all lose.

As managers, we are responsible for not letting you fail, unless you are hell-bent on doing so, in which case we're not going to stand in your way. If we hire a new security guard and the security fails, we've *all* got to take the heat. If my new golf professional is alienating some of the members, we're *all* going to suffer. If my new restaurant manager is great with the members but terrible with the staff, I'm going to hear about it. And if everything runs smoothly, I'll be happy even if I don't hear about it.

GOOD EMPLOYEE RULE 2:
Everybody on our team has to appreciate everyone else's job.

I don't want any of my employees ever to say, or ever to think, "That's not my job." The minute somebody says that, he's out.

Approach every task as an opportunity to show us that you are ready and eager to learn and grow. Don't think of it as work—think of it as an opportunity to better yourself.

GOOD EMPLOYEE RULE 3:
You've got to want to be there.

If you don't want to come to work in the morning, do us a favor: don't show up. Don't worry about us, we'll find someone who does want to come in. Remember that job interview you just aced? Well, you're not the only fish in the sea.

GOOD EMPLOYEE RULE 4:
Be in the know.

I want everybody who works for me to know *who* they are working for, *what* they are working for, *what* our mutual goal is. That "in the know" feeling has to be transmitted every day and every night, through every echelon of the organization, so that it filters down to the members and guests and creates an atmosphere of belonging, which is the sure sign of a top-notch, highly functional organization.

GOOD EMPLOYEE RULE 5:
Bring me a solution, not a problem.

One of my more recent recruits is a terrific guy. He's smart, dedicated, motivated, talented. But he's been learning the Good Employee Rule 5 a little too slowly for my taste. He still has a tendency to present me with long, drawn-out scenarios. Whether by fax, phone, or e-mail, it's always the same: too lengthy, too involved, not enough actionable bullet points to help me make a decision, let alone not a decision already made, awaiting a quick review and my signature.

The other day he called to tell me he had a problem.

"Okay," I said. "What do you need to fix it?"

"We may need to purchase a new piece of equipment, but I'm not sure."

"What does it cost?"

"I don't have a number yet."

"Get the information, and either e-mail me or call me."

Later that day a four-page essay came to my office by fax. I looked it over quickly and didn't see any numbers, so I called him.

"Ray," I said, "what does it cost?"

"I just sent you the fax."

"Ray," I said, holding my temper, "I don't have the *time* to look at that fax. Why do you need this product, and what's it going to cost?"

"Sixty-five thousand dollars."

"Ray, in one sentence, why do you need it?"

He hemmed and hawed, and finally came out with "Let me get back to you on that."

My assistant manager called me up later that day and said, "Carolyn, I was right there when he fed in that fax. It was too late for me to stop it. I said, 'You can't do this to Carolyn. . . . She's a three-minute girl; you've got to get the information to her *in one page.*'"

Please don't just bring me a problem. Don't say, "Carolyn, we've got a water leak on the fourth hole." I'd much prefer "We've got a water leak. I've contacted the irrigation company. He's on his way, and he expects it will take him about an hour to fix. Bottom line, I think we're looking at an expenditure of five hundred dollars. I'll keep you posted if it runs any higher."

I appreciate, by the way, being made aware of the problem. But I would much rather be made aware of a workable solution. I'm not saying that every problem can be solved without input from above. But if it can be, *do it.*

Which leads me directly to:

GOOD EMPLOYEE RULE 6:
When in doubt, make a decision and stand by it.

Analyze the problem yourself. Have enough confidence to say to me, "Here is my recommendation. I've looked into it, and I know what I'm talking about."

If you simply can't reach a decision on your own, break the range of responses down into, at most, three action scenarios. I prefer a strong recommendation, with reasons and price tag attached. Taking a risk that you might be wrong is the only way to rise in this organization. Remember, the best way to be a good employee is to act like a manager.

So, you've taken a shot. You've researched the costs. You've played out the different scenarios. You've made every conceivable projection in your head. What have you just done? Without knowing it, you've applied:

GOOD EMPLOYEE RULE 7:
Become an expert in your field.

"It's okay for someone to give you advice," I recently told one of my employees, who was complaining to me about getting pushed around by a nonexpert who just happened to have a higher rank in the organization. "But if somebody starts shoving some bad advice down your throat and you have more experience and more education in this topic, keep in mind that you don't have to defer to somebody else's opinion just because they happen to be three steps above you on the corporate ladder."

It all goes back to being the master of your domain. Only by knowing everything you need to know—and more, if possible—about your own field can you expect us to have the confidence that you are ready to take the next step. And only after you have become an expert in your field can you even contemplate developing expertise in other areas. This is all about anticipating your next move, and persuading us to give you the opportunity to grow. In order to move up, you need to show us two things:

1. You have your present job nailed.
2. You know enough about some areas outside your immediate field to advance to the next level.

Asking for a Raise or a Promotion

So you've followed my advice to the letter and learned all the lessons. You've minded your P's and Q's and handled all the Do's and Don'ts. What has happened? You've done a great job, that's what happened, and now you are definitely in line for a raise, a promotion, or maybe even the jackpot: both. But you're not sure how to ask me for one. Here's some advice: don't hang back.

Make your pitch.

Here's how.

Let's just say that I myself have asked for a raise or promotion both the right way and the wrong way a few times. A few years ago, when I was given the Bedminster golf property to manage in addition to Trump National, I saw it as a reasonable opportunity to ask Donald Trump for a raise. As you can imagine, this is not the easiest thing to get up the gumption to do. And I knew that the cardinal rule in these situations has two important parts:

1. Correctly anticipate the most likely reaction to your request.
2. Anticipate your next move.

Donald Trump says that, in this situation, "Timing is everything." In my case, the timing seemed fine, although in retrospect, I can see that was where I committed my first error. As I tend to do with Mr. Trump, I got straight to the point. I told him I thought I deserved a raise. I didn't delve into the details, and he didn't ask. I know some people believe it's best to put these requests in memo form. Personally, I tend to subscribe to the notion that if you are in line for a raise or a promotion you don't need four pages citing your accomplishments—all it should take is a verbal reminder of how good you are. If he or she doesn't know that already, you've not been doing a good job of selling yourself to your superior.

I took Mr. Trump's grunt as an assent that he and I agreed I deserved a raise. But that was only half the battle. For the second phase of my operation, I threw him a curveball without meaning to. Without prompting, I tossed out the number I was looking for. In response, he looked me square in the eye. "Let me think about it," he replied calmly, "and I'll get back to you."

I was totally taken aback. I had been all primed to play the negotiation game. I would go in with a high number, he would come back with a low number, and then we would talk and end up somewhere in the middle.

But I had made, I suddenly realized, a false assumption about how Donald Trump would act. By classifying him in my mind as Mr. Decisive and Mr. Negotiator, I had failed to anticipate the fact that, as Warren Buffett says about investing, "You don't need to swing at every pitch." My biggest failure had been to assume that Mr. Trump's response would be predictable. I should never have expected predictability from Donald Trump.

So I was surprised. And as both a manager and an employee, I hate few things more than surprises. Now I had to do a better job of entering into my boss's mind. What was Donald Trump doing? What was he thinking? What message was he seeking to convey to me by failing to respond?

What he was doing without really saying so, I decided, was letting me know that he was surprised by the number. He hadn't been surprised by the request itself, but he had been surprised by its size. Okay, I decided, the right number would have been one that he *wouldn't* have had to think so hard about. In fact, by failing to hand him a more reasonable number, I had broken one of my own cardinal rules: I had brought him a problem, not a solution. I had given him a headache as opposed to relieving one. What was Donald Trump's goal in this negotiation? A number that would make both of us happy.

CAROLYN 101:

Asking for a raise of more than a small percentage of
your base salary is a major step, to be contemplated only
if you truly believe your new position requires either
significantly more work or that much more responsibility
than your present position.

I now had a decision to make. If he didn't get back to me, I
could get back to him. One of my personal guidelines was that
no way was I going to lose face with Donald Trump. I wasn't
going to backpedal, at least not to his face. It occurred to me
that I had also neglected to realize that while I had been given
a promotion, to managing the Bedminster, New Jersey, property in addition to the Briarcliff Manor, New York, property, I
hadn't yet proven myself in the new position. Faulty timing
had been my original error, and coming on too strong with
the number had simply compounded it.

So what were my options? I had already rejected admitting
that I was in the wrong—at least by coming right out and
saying so. Mr. Trump had sent me a very important signal by
not rejecting my request out of hand. But instead, very deliberately I had to assume, he had said he would think about it.
What I could infer from that statement was that he regarded
my request not as totally off the wall but rather as premature
and overblown, and he wanted me to know it.

For the longest time, I did nothing. For six months, I waited for him to respond. But he didn't. All right, I said to myself, he is teaching me a lesson, like a Zen master, pointing toward something I need to learn. Or, just possibly, he forgot about it.

I eventually got that raise—it just took me longer than originally anticipated. What it took, in fact, was time. I decided that what I needed to do to demonstrate that I had proven myself as the operator of the additional property was to wait for some profit-and-loss numbers to come in, to justify my own number.

I went in with a new number, lower but not a lot lower than my previous one. I didn't openly address my performance at Bedminster, because he knew the particulars already. What I did do—very deliberately—was to act as if we were starting this discussion from scratch, and that for the purposes of this meeting, the previous meeting had never happened.

Since I was the one who had made the original error, I took it upon myself to come up with a number that I could feel confident we would both be happy with. The actual request was nothing compared to the preparation that went into it. I made my request. He granted it. From his tone I could tell that he appreciated my revised approach.

Asking for a Raise or Promotion Don'ts

1. Come in after you've been working for me for a year and say, "I've been here for a year and I deserve a raise."

2. Come to me with a song and dance about how the

competition gets paid more than you do. I once had a secretary tell me, "Carolyn, I've being doing a little research, and a lot of executive secretaries are making *x*, and I'm not there."

I would reply to both such requests, "Why don't you think about a few *real* reasons why *you're* deserving of a raise?"

Asking for a Raise or Promotion Do's

1. Make a strong case that you are worth it. Explain in detail to me what your contribution has been to the group's success. A rising tide lifts all boats, and if you've done good for the organization, your boss wants to hear it. As I said before, some people say you should put your case for a raise or promotion into writing, so that your boss can use it as a set of talking points with his or her superiors. In some corporate settings that might be useful, but the day I have to start sending my boss memos telling him or her why I am doing a good job is the day I start sending out résumés myself!

2. When building that case, present me with a plan for your promotion. Once again, do the work yourself. As in "I've been doing this job for such-and-such period of time, during which time I have accomplished these particular goals. I see the next reasonable step as tackling these responsibilities in the future, so that we can

all accomplish the following objectives." Show me you've thought about where you're going with the organization.

Some Examples of What Will Get Me to Fire You

Much as it might surprise you in light of my role on *The Apprentice*, I hate firing people. To all of us at The Trump Organization, every firing feels like a personal failure. But every once in a while you might either hire or promote someone who doesn't work out, and it becomes clear to you that to keep that person in his or her present position is a detriment to the rest of the staff, as well as to the organization as a whole. When that realization strikes, it's usually too late for the employee to mount a self-rescue operation. You see it in *The Apprentice* boardroom—how often does someone who's been told they're fired get to reverse the decision on appeal?

Letting somebody go is one of the toughest decisions that any manager can make. But in a few cases, saying "You're fired" becomes a no-brainer. Here are two things you can do to get me to fire you.

BAD EMPLOYEE MISTAKE 1:
Have an unhealthy attitude.

The dividing line between self-confidence and attitude is often painfully thin. The real difference, I've found, between having a healthy dose of self-confidence and having an attitude problem is that truly self-confident people are generally confident enough to withstand and even absorb constructive criticism. But people who have an attitude generally buckle under criticism and make their insecurity known by becoming more arrogant, more defensive, more abrasive. When this occurs, I can virtually guarantee an unhappy outcome.

A few years ago I hired a young woman as a restaurant manager. She had an excellent résumé and made a strong impression in her interview. She had an upbeat and engaging personality, which I could tell would make one of the most important aspects of her job—dealing with the members— easy for her and easy for them. She was about twenty-five, tall and blond and obviously eager and ambitious. The one negative I noted was, beneath her self-confidence, a whiff of an attitude. By which I mean an unhealthy attitude.

CAROLYN 101:

A bad apple with a bad attitude can compromise the team.

In this woman's case, I sensed an unwillingness to get her hands dirty, to take on any tasks that she deemed beneath her. But she was far and away the best qualified of the candidates. The possibility that she might have an attitude gave me pause, but I decided to hire her anyway, under the assumption that the attitude might drop away when she started working with my great team.

As I had anticipated, she was terrific when dealing with the

– 132 –

members. She engaged them as if they were old friends without being too familiar. But she treated her staff the completely opposite way, as if they weren't worthy of her respect.

As her manager, I was faced with a decision: I could do nothing and let her subordinates down. Or I could have an honest talk with her about her attitude and its negative repercussions.

So I called her in for a heart-to-heart. I told her that, much as I appreciated her skill and ease with the members, it was critically important to extend that same attitude toward her staff, because when the chips were down those were the people she was going to need to call upon for support. Those relationships, I stressed, were at least as high value as the member relations. And I reminded her that it wasn't always the easy part of the job that was worth focusing on, but the parts that called for improvement.

As I should have suspected she would, she immediately became haughty and caustic. She did everything she could to convey the message that she did not regard herself as my subordinate. Still, having told her what I needed to tell her, I gave her the benefit of the doubt and let her go off to think it over, hoping she would see the error of her ways.

What she chose to do instead was ignore my advice and start obsessing over whether her contract would be renewed for the following season. She asked for another meeting with me at which, instead of being contrite, she demanded a specific date for her seasonal termination or renewal. She seemed utterly oblivious to the fact that she was sabotaging herself by trying to force me to make a decision on rehiring her when her performance was in question. One of the problems with having an attitude is that it tends to make you a little out of touch with reality.

"I'm not going to give you an answer right now," I said, which was actually in her best interest, since I was inclined to let her go at this point. This is when she really crossed the line, asking me to sign a contract committing to bringing her back. Believe it or not, she also requested a raise! I had no choice but to let her go. Here's why:

- She had failed to realize that her job required a wide set of interpersonal skills in addition to functional skills. She had some of the interpersonal skills she needed to perform the job effectively nailed, but not the others. You have to have the whole package if you're going to do your job right.
- She had failed to take constructive criticism. When I had reasonably approached her with a suggestion for improvement, she had rejected it as hostile. She could have decided to learn and change. Instead, she chose to cling to her weaknesses in the erroneous belief that they were strengths.
- She had failed to make an accurate assessment of her strategic position. She had somehow developed the impression that her position was untouchable. But in fact, as someone with a position that requires rehiring, she was considerably more vulnerable than your average employee.

BAD EMPLOYEE MISTAKE 2:
Fail to show up.

A year or so later, I had a controller who stopped coming in to work regularly. He started out by taking days off. After he ran out of sick days and personal days, he began showing up late. He made all kinds of lame excuses for his behavior, but it got me, his employer, wondering if he was interviewing for other jobs. You don't want your boss wondering these things about you.

After a short period of time, I decided to level with him. "If you're not going to be doing this job, please tell me now."

"Oh no, I can do it," he assured me. "These recent absences were an aberration."

Now I had a decision to make. On the one hand, an employee who barely shows up over a two-week period is asking to be fired. On the other hand, in his particular case, he had been able to maintain a reasonable standard of performance despite his protracted absences. I could have decided to focus only on his work product, and ignore the problem of his hours. But that would have created an additional problem: giving an impression that at Trump National we tolerated chronic absenteeism.

We take *The Good Employee Rule # 3: You've Got to Want to Be There* very seriously, and even in those rare cases when employees might be able to do a full day's job with a half day's work, we need all employees to realize that not every job permits that flexibility.

I gave him a week to clean up his act. But things didn't get better after our discussion. If anything, they got worse. He kept taking days off, without explanation, and one day he didn't show up just happened to be payroll day. When he had the gall to come to claim his check, I let him know it was the last one he'd be seeing from me.

What he did to get me to fire him was comprised of two parts:

- He was repeatedly absent.
- He lied and broke his promise after we gave him a second chance.

CAROLYN 101:

If you are not going to come in on Friday, don't bother showing up on Monday.

BAD EMPLOYEE MISTAKE 3:
Fail to swim when we drop you in the water.

I recently had to make one of the most difficult decisions of my career. At Trump National we have an informal philosophy of helping people make the stretch, grow into new situations. But in some cases we promote people too quickly. Since we can't keep them in positions of incompetence until they grow into their jobs, sometimes we have to fire them.

We all liked this young man so much that I fear we might

have allowed those positive feelings to influence unduly our decision to promote him. Because we were so proud of him, we might have missed out on the fact that he wasn't mature enough to handle the job.

Jordan Pope was twenty-five when we promoted him to a senior position in our administration. His first mistake was the common one of failing to grasp the importance of the pro-bationary period. Rather than show us that he was young and hungry, this otherwise highly intelligent young man gave us the impression that, most of all, he liked hanging around with the big boys. And I mean hanging around. As their newly ap-pointed manager and being younger than his subordinates, he should have shown his staff that not only did he not mind a bit getting down in the trenches with them but he actually en-joyed it. But what our young friend began doing instead was cruising and coasting.

CAROLYN 101:

**Just because you've risen through the ranks,
don't believe you've paid your dues.**

In fact, this amiable young man's dues-paying period was just beginning. But rather than tucking in and handling every detail of his job meticulously, he began delegating his respon-sibilities a little too laxly.

The straw that broke the camel's back for me was when he

headed out of town over the Fourth of July weekend, a critical opening weekend in the golf business. He compounded his error by not bothering to check with me about it. I suspect he knew I would not approve. It wouldn't have been like me to deny him leave to attend a family weekend. But it would have been like me to explain that this was a grave tactical error in his probation period, the one that would get us watching him more closely and make us wise to how little he was actually doing. He didn't last long after that.

Where had he gone wrong?

- He had failed to understand that his position was a probationary promotion, not a done deal. He could still blow it, and he did.
- He had failed to value this promotion as the opportunity it was, to show us that he could master this new situation.
- He had drawn too much attention to what he wasn't doing rather than what he was.

CAROLYN 101:

In a new job, show me what you've done, not what you chose not to do.

The good employee is a knowing employee. If you're looking for us to hire you, we want you to know something about us. More specifically, we need you to know exactly what you can do for us, and that it is something we need to get done. Once you've accomplished that task and we have hired you, we need you to learn everything that there is to know about your job. We need you to become the expert in your field. And then, while you're becoming an expert in your field, we need you to start anticipating your next move, which involves becoming an expert in other fields.

Now, we need you to know just what it will take to make promoting you a no-brainer for us. And when we do promote you, as we certainly will if you have done all the above, you need to repeat the same process all over again. At a certain point, that knowing employee becomes a knowing manager. Then, the manager of other managers. In virtually every organization, there's plenty of opportunity to move up. You just need to know how to get there.

FIVE

The Managerial Mother

To: Carolyn Kepcher [E-mail]

I really like watching your show, and you've become one of my favorite people on *The Apprentice*. I was surprised to read in *People* that you are a mother of two! How do you juggle your job and at the same time the responsibilities of family and motherhood? All of us have seen you guys pull some very late hours.

Motherhood Is Not a Day Job

By 4:30 on the afternoon of June 16, 2000, I had been lying in the maternity ward at White Plains Hospital for twelve hours. I had been in active labor for over an hour, and after an hour more of concentrated pushing, the baby still wasn't making much progress and a potentially serious complication had arisen: he and I had started to spike a high fever. Soon afterward, on doctors' orders, our son, Connor, was delivered by emergency cesarean section.

After the birth, when the baby had fallen asleep, my husband, George, dashed out and returned with a pizza and a couple of cold beers. I hadn't had a sip of anything alcoholic since getting pregnant, and that bottle of beer tasted terrific. The pizza went down like a meal catered by the Four Seasons. Looking back, realizing now how unaware I was of the balancing act to come and the adjustment it would require, I know how precious that rare moment of peace was.

I now had a new life, in more ways than one: a new life sleeping peacefully beside me in my bed, and a new life that incorporated all of our separate lives into a new rhythm, with new joys, new surprises, new demands. I had done all I could to think about what might lie ahead. Now, it dawned upon me that I would have to stop thinking, and start living, from day to day. That would probably be the greatest surprise I would be forced to contend with as a new mother: life involved something more than being quick on my feet and planning ahead. I would need to roll with and react to an often bewildering multiplicity of forces which, in that brief silent moment, I could barely comprehend.

Immediately, George began delivering the good news by phone, starting out with parents, siblings, cousins, and other relatives. I was too exhausted to speak with anyone that evening. At my request he placed our first colleague call to Norma Foerderer, Donald Trump's longtime executive assistant and my dear and close friend. Of all the people I have come to know and admire during my decade with The Trump Organization, Norma has been my Rock of Gibraltar. She radiates a natural grace and elegance to which I can only aspire. I think people who know both of us can detect a strong influence of Norma on the calm, cool, collected Carolyn you see on the small screen. I knew she would be thrilled and pass the news along to Mr. Trump for me.

At some ungodly hour the next morning, the phone on my bedside table rang.

"It's Donald Trump. How are you feeling?"

I was so touched. It was our first call of the day, and just because he's always up several hours before anyone else on the planet—with the possible exception of military jet pilots on patrol—doesn't mean he deserves any less credit for being first! After I'd assured him that we were all fine and Connor dandy, he slipped into a business discussion without realizing it. Being polite, I repeated "uh-huh, uh-huh" into the phone, still exhausted from labor. At some point he caught himself and quickly switched gears back to the personal. I could hear the guilt in his voice—he was clearly thinking, "My gosh, this woman is recovering from surgery, and here am I talking to her about the golf course construction!"

Although I didn't say so, I couldn't have been happier about the golf course construction, which I thought was exquisitely timed to coincide with Connor's birth. We had recently won our zoning approvals, and within weeks the first Trump Organization shovel would hit Briarcliff Manor dirt and the long-awaited construction would begin. The sprawling old clubhouse was due to come down and be replaced by a multi-million-dollar extravaganza. The old course was going to be entirely ripped out and a new course installed on a site that had been significantly expanded through land acquisition to accommodate a larger driving range and many more yards of fairway.

Because of all this demolition and construction, we were not going to be opening the club for the summer season. The happy coincidence with Connor's birth meant that I would be granted a certain degree of "flextime" without having to ask for it, and that was going to make a tough situation tolerable.

It was during that phone conversation with Mr. Trump that I understood the magnitude of the challenge I was facing. This wasn't going to be a day at the beach. Sometimes, I knew, I was going to feel wired, tired, frazzled, and torn. Between my husband of six years, my boss of eight years, and my son of two hours, I could feel confident that at any point of my day and night, one if not all of these guys would be posing demands on my time and attention that would make accommodating it all without friction seem like a pipe dream.

But today, nearly five years, two golf courses, and one lovely little girl later, I can safely say that, like so many difficult challenges I've faced in my life, one of the great things about striving to strike a reasonable balance between work life and home life is how amazing it feels when—once in a blue moon—you finally sense you're getting it right!

Assigning Supporting Roles

Trying to strike that balance between work and home life is, as we all know, the stuff of Hollywood comedies like *Baby Boom* and *Nine to Five*. That the primary burden of this struggle tends to fall on working women more than on their husbands is not a matter in much dispute. From my perspective as a working mother, it all boils down to one thing: *support*.

If you're going to do this and do it well, you're going to need to count on loads of support from every direction: support from your boss, support from your spouse, support from your staff, kids, friends, neighbors, extended family, and colleagues. And don't forget support from yourself.

Support from Above

I had waited until I was six months pregnant before telling Donald that I was expecting. He knew that George and I had been married for six years, and that we were eventually going to start a family. So, while I felt mildly anxious about telling him, I was confident it wouldn't come as a huge surprise, and I was also excited about sharing our good news. As a proud and committed father himself, I fully expected he would be happy for me.

That said, I decided to wait until I was showing (slightly) before dropping the news on him. And I decided to present the information in such a way as to assure him that disruption to my work life would be minimal. We were winding down a meeting in his office when I said, very casually, "By the way, I'm going to need to take some time off in about three months."

"Okay," he said, "you've been working hard. Everybody needs a break."

"Well, actually, I'll be needing to make a little trip to the hospital."

Immediately, he looked concerned. "Are you all right? Is there anything I can do?"

I could tell he was puzzled because I was smiling.

"It's a standard procedure . . . I'm going to give birth!" I said matter-of-factly.

He burst into a grin. He couldn't have been happier for me.

We didn't discuss any concerns about whether it might prove difficult for me to keep up with everything at the club with a new baby at home. Although I never asked, I think that he simply assumed I was a competent person, and one way or another, we'd handle it.

Support by Your Side

Most of us are not raised to think much about how our careers will fit into our home life. In school and college, we tend to focus on areas of scholastic aptitude and interest, and simply assume that the rest will take care of itself. But how many of us who yearn in early life to be musicians, physicians, artists, or astronauts spend any time considering how those careers fit in with marriage, family, and children if we want them? I don't mean to suggest that you should pick a career on this basis, but you should have a game plan so that life doesn't entirely pass you by and you miss out on some of the things you wanted.

CAROLYN 101:

**When planning your career, don't forget to consider
how a family will fit into it if you want one.**

Not a day of my life goes by that I don't thank my lucky stars I met George Kepcher when I did. From the very beginning of our relationship, we both knew that an important part of our bond would be to support each other in achieving our dreams, no matter where those dreams and ambitions might take us.

An important part of our relationship has always been a strong appreciation of the value of the working mother. I can also count myself fortunate to have been raised in a family where my mother's working outside the home not only didn't raise an eyebrow but generated pride. Just as my father never minded that my mother brought home a paycheck—in fact, he appreciated it—George has made it clear that he understands and supports the self-esteem and satisfaction that women who do choose to work outside the home derive from their careers.

CAROLYN 101:

For anyone looking to get married and work full-time after having children: *Pick your spouse carefully!* It's essential to discuss how you each feel about this issue, which can have a lot more bearing on your relationship than you realize.

Not long after George and I met—on a Metro North train heading from Dobbs Ferry to Grand Central Terminal en route to a Paul Simon concert in Central Park—I "graduated" from the restaurant in Dobbs Ferry and got my first job at the Beekman Tower Hotel. By the time George and I were married, I had been promoted to manager of the Zephyr Grill there, where the hours were brutal. I can't even count how many nights I ended up staying so late that, rather than risk the long drive home, I would take a room at the hotel and crash there. George, who is in the construction industry, where the hours tend to be a trifle more regular, simply had to reconcile himself to the fact that in the restaurant, resort, and hospitality industry, working nights and weekends is not extraordinary but ordinary.

But what complemented this schedule discrepancy nicely is that when we bought our first house, he was able to spend those weekends fixing up and rebuilding practically from scratch. How's that for a matching set?

So George knew precisely what he was getting into when he married me. I couldn't help it if a strong work ethic had been bred into my bones. Fortunately for our marriage, one of the many things that binds us is that we share this work ethic. While there are certainly plenty of men who might have felt threatened by, envious of, or angry about my ambition and drive, George Kepcher felt none of those things. I can sincerely say that the emotion he most honestly felt as I made my way up the ladder was pride, unalloyed and unconditional. And as we moved into this new phase of our lives, I knew that I could count on George to be the father to our children when they needed him, and that there would be times when he would be handling that responsibility alone.

I had total trust that he would be up to the job.

Support from Your Staff

With some trepidation, I returned to work at the Trump National Golf Club—still a work in progress—after a three-week maternity leave. To those of you who think that three months sounds short, three weeks must sound stunningly brief. And so it was. But it was also, for me, a rare, precious break from a life that from the age of twelve on had been so dominated by work. Those blissful days were a special time for me and Connor, and instead of going to meetings and reviewing budgets, I happily occupied myself fixing bottles and folding booties. I so loved the time I had with Connor, but all too quickly it vanished into thin air.

I could never have even considered taking those three weeks—much less made it through the succeeding months, when my occasionally precarious balancing act required continual adjustments to get it right—without the solid support of my superior staff. Everything I wrote in the previous chapter about the value of hiring great employees was proven to me during this period. What they did to support me was very simple: They relied on themselves to the maximum extent possible.

Support at Home

I have never subscribed to the notion that the mother is by some divine right destined to be a child's sole caregiver. Yes, the mother clearly plays a primary role. But if you want or need to work outside the home after your child is born, it helps to divest yourself of that all too common notion "I need to be everything to this baby." The concept so widely accepted in the United States and many Western countries that the mother should be a child's sole source of emotional support is extremely culturally conditioned. In fact, in many if not most other cultures, grandparents, uncles and aunts, cousins, nephews and nieces, and other members of the extended family—even close friends—play a significant role in child rearing.

When you are promoted from employee to manager, often the most difficult lesson to learn is delegating authority. What you need to do, in effect, is trust other people to carry out the decisions you would make if you were on the scene yourself, or had the time. Now, imagine what it's like to delegate the care of your newborn.

The first day I had to leave Connor and drive back to work

was wrenching. But our mutual separation anxiety was made somewhat more manageable by the fact that we had been blessed with a wonderful, competent, loving babysitter, whom I trusted implicitly. She became a critical element in my support system.

When hiring a babysitter, I applied the same rules I use to hire an employee at work: I looked for someone I could trust and feel confident would behave precisely as I would in every conceivable situation—particularly in an emergency.

We were enormously fortunate that we already had someone within the Kepcher organization who had been handling minor housekeeping chores for us for a number of years and was ready to move up to a full-time babysitting position. So we were spared the complexities of taking out ads, working with placement agencies, or interviewing total strangers. This woman was far from a total stranger, and she was eager to become part of our team.

I realized that if we went through an agency, we might have had an enormous number of qualified babysitting candidates to choose from. But just as I do when hiring an employee at work, I preferred the intuitive to the analytical approach. I suppose I could have gone looking for someone with a degree in early childhood development, or years of experience and a list of references as long as your arm. I didn't do any of that. Instead, I looked for The Click. After all, this was my most critical hire ever.

My primary criterion was to find someone warm, caring, and giving. That she loved our son and he loved her was obviously what mattered most. And that actually took some getting used to—I had the not unreasonable fear that my son would end up loving the babysitter more than he loved me. It was certainly true that when he was in the mood for a sweet treat, he knew who to look to—and it wasn't me! My advice to new working mothers with this fear is that no one, in the end, can ever replace a mother's or a father's love.

CAROLYN 101:

Your role as a working mother is to be a good manager
both at home and at work. Set clear expectations.
Establish a routine. Be organized. Communicate effectively.
Offer praise. Often, the same rules that
apply at work apply at home.

For Many of Us, Work Is Not a Choice

With the high cost of living today, it's not easy (except in the very uppermost tax brackets) for one working spouse, no matter how hardworking or successful, to support a whole family in the lifestyle to which many of us would like to become accustomed. So for those who struggle to maintain a middle-class lifestyle, a two-career family is not a choice but a necessity. This is one reason that I find society's tendency to make working and motherhood a moral issue, a matter of strict rights and wrongs and certain family values, counterproductive. It's a question not so much of getting it "right" in any objective sense but of getting it to feel right to you.

CAROLYN 101:

Balancing work and home life is not a moral issue. No one but you has any right to say whether what you are doing is good or bad.

Much recent research on work and family points unassailably to the conclusion that it is usually not the *fact* that both parents work that has a negative impact on marriage and children. It is rather the reality that so many parents and spouses who feel overburdened by work tend unwittingly to bring negative feelings home with them. What matters most is that when we experience periods of stress at work, we do our best to leave those feelings at the office.

Making Work Work

Coping with the emotional issues of separation became my number one task after I returned to work from maternity leave. I did all the usual things that first-time working mothers do, which I learned are things that really work:

- I plastered pictures of the baby all over my office.
- I called the babysitter as many times as I needed to.
- I drove home at lunch hour.
- I occasionally brought the baby to the office.

I was fortunate to have hired a wonderful assistant, who gave the term "support" a new meaning. Without having to ask, she simply knew when I needed to take time at home with Connor, and I couldn't even count the times that she brought me work that needed to get done at a point when I simply needed to be home.

But what really made the transitional experience work for me was the fact that the club was closed and the course under construction. This meant I could more often bring Connor into work with me, and no one would really be disturbed. I could park him just about anywhere in his portable play-pen and—particularly when he slept, which in those days was most of the time—actually get a fair amount of work done. If I needed to go dashing off, someone on my staff was happy to keep an eye on him until I got back.

Little Connor became quite the regular as the Trump National Golf Club took shape before our eyes. It seemed some-how fitting that I was able to bring my new child into my spot, where an entire green new little world was being born. My staff and I concentrated on creating a membership to the new club, which I must say took some imagination on both our parts and those of the prospective members, since the whole place was a work in progress.

During those early weeks of summer, before it got too hot, I fell into the habit of parking Connor outside, where I could have informal conferences with my staff overlooking the course in progress. One day I was signing a stack of invoices when Donald Trump came up and began talking to me about something. With some amusement I took note of the fact that he clearly hadn't registered my son's presence in the playpen.

Mr. Trump was somewhere in midsentence when a gurgling sound emanated from the portable playpen behind the table, and he stopped short and looked around, as if he thought he might be hearing things. I watched his eyes fall to the source of the sound and his mouth break into a wide smile. "Connor!" he cried out, remembering my son's name—which I appreciated. They'd never met, so I had the pleasure of introducing two of the most important men in my life to each other. Donald Trump clearly couldn't have been happier to meet Connor Kepcher. And if my boss was the least bit surprised to see my son lying there, outside my office, he certainly never let on. My feeling was that he regarded Connor's temporary presence on my skeleton sales staff as an asset as opposed to a liability.

Once again, Mr. Trump's sales acumen proved superlative. One afternoon a few days later, a young couple came to look around the facility. Although it wasn't as if I always took my son into work—not by a long shot—by coincidence I had Connor with me that day. As the prospective members and I set off on our tour, I cheerfully snatched him up, gently inserted him into the crook of my arm, and carried him as we walked. I could tell by the expressions on our visitors' faces that they got quite a kick out of our little fourth wheel. I will never be sure, because they never said so, but I think Connor's presence—that personal sales touch!—might have closed the deal. They signed up on the spot and have been happy members ever since.

Back to Business

Planning the grand opening of all eighteen holes of Trump National took more than six months. But it was also a day for which I had spent the previous six years in active preparation. Our gala was a smashing success, attended by just about every A-list golf journalist in the country, in addition to any number of golfing celebrities, including the talk show host Regis Philbin, the actor-director-producer Ron Howard, the broadcaster Ernie Anastos, Bobby Bonilla of the Mets, and the comedian Robert Klein. A special martini was even created for the occasion! I can only assume it was as delicious as it looked, because I was banned from sampling it, by both state law and doctor's orders. That's because I was eight months pregnant with a second child, our daughter, Cassidy.

They say that in so many ways your second child is easier than your first. And it is certainly true that, the second time around, one tends to know an enormous amount more about what to do than with one's first. But life after our second child became much more intense and complicated for me. Because even if things were quieting down to some extent on the home front, they were rapidly heating up at work.

With Trump National open for business every day except Monday—when we typically had our golf outings—I felt an enormous urgency both about returning to work and about sticking around there as much as I could. I knew it would be up to me to hit the ground running. This time around, I was able to plan my time a little more carefully. Since during the golf season I generally have to work weekends, George takes care of the kids on most of those Saturdays and Sundays. He goes out of his way to make these days fun for them, whether it's taking a trip to Great Adventure or just playing in our backyard.

I in turn made my free Mondays special "Mommy and Connor Days," when I would drive Connor to school in the morning, pick him up around noon, and take him to lunch and then for a special treat, perhaps a trip to the zoo or the aquarium or even just a little walk around our town, while our babysitter stayed home with Cassidy.

I also learned to do a better job of integrating our family rhythms with my work rhythms. Since we have months during the winter when the club is closed, I used those periods to spend extra time with the kids. Simple as these innovations might sound, implementing them took a certain amount of planning and follow-through. I was beginning to think I had this work-home balance down pat.

Until, that is, only a few days after my return from Cassidy's birth, I took a phone call from Donald Trump.

"I have a few questions about the Bedminster property," he started out.

Bedminster? I had no idea what he was talking about, but I listened closely, took down a few notes regarding his concerns, and told him I'd get back to him later that day with the information he needed. After hanging up, I shouted over to a member of my staff, "Did we just buy a golf course in Bedminster, New Jersey?"

That's how I heard that, during my three-week leave of absence, Mr. Trump had bought a property in Bedminster, New Jersey, a member-owned golf property that had fallen on hard times, which we were offering to bail out of its debts by taking it over. If they didn't accept our proposal, the current membership was likely to face a hefty assessment to clear those debts.

Soon after that phone call, Mr. Trump got around to letting me know that he wanted me to run it. Bedminster too. Right then and there the old work-life balance equation presented itself in starker terms than I had imagined. Yes, I had gotten a lot better at negotiating the dividing lines between professional time and personal time. But with Bedminster a work in progress and Briarcliff Manor up and running, I had my hands full.

It had simply been assumed by senior management (that is, Donald Trump) that I would accept these new responsibilities in the same gung-ho, can-do spirit with which I had received every promotion up until then. No one had really thought about the fact that I had a newborn girl on my hands, in addition to a fast-growing son who was full of new challenges daily.

Doing what I do in a situation like this, I sat myself down and reviewed my options. One option, of course, would be to turn down responsibility for the Bedminster property—along with the promotion and raise that would probably go with it. I could choose to tell Donald Trump, "You know, I've got two kids now, and I just can't work the way I used to. I don't think I can handle it."

I think you know me well enough by now to realize that that would never happen. Frankly, saying no to Mr. Trump's offer to give me another leg up was never a choice I seriously considered. Instead, I decided to think about how I could handle the new load without driving myself and my family right up the wall. Throughout the fall, as the golf season wound down, I found myself wrestling interminably with the financial issues raised by the Bedminster buyout. I was beginning to wonder whether life was only going to get busier. And in this regard, my concerns were well founded.

CAROLYN 101:

Sometimes, when too many tasks overwhelm you,
you've got to take life like a Chinese restaurant—
one item from column A, one from column B—
until you're done for the day.

True Stories from the Life of a Multitasking Mom

By the fall of 2002, I was operating Trump National in Briar-cliff Manor, New York (which now included overseeing the construction and sales of residential villas), operating Trump National in Bedminster, New Jersey, and raising the Kepcher kids with strong support from a great home team. Some days I felt very torn, and I have to say that some mornings, pulling out of the driveway with my little girl screaming "Mommy! Mommy!" didn't make that drive to work any easier.

On more than one occasion I barely squeaked by. One recent morning my daughter was having a bad diaper day. After I changed her, and some of the mess got on my new clean shirt, I changed shirts. Not five minutes later my son came running over to say good-bye. Between the diaper and the new shirt, I had neglected to notice that he'd developed a nasty nosebleed. While I cleaned up his face, we got some of his blood on my shirt. Okay, I said to myself, I've got another clean shirt around here somewhere. I changed shirts again. I was running a little late now, and grabbed my commuter cup of coffee. While I was taking a quick sip as I screeched out of the driveway, the hot coffee spilled all over my pants. And so I had to go back into the house, say hello to the kids and the babysitter, run upstairs, and change into a clean pair of pants. I wasn't a hundred yards down the road when I realized that I'd forgotten my cell phone. I turned back around, went into the house for a second time, upset both my children by returning and leaving so quickly, and made it to work a half hour late.

CAROLYN 101:

Whether you like it or not, there are going to be those moments and those days. Do your best not to be too thrown by them. That only makes it worse.

But I had learned to do a better job of drawing firm lines between my work life and my home life. I made a point of compartmentalizing my life more clearly. For instance,

- I took almost no work calls at home.
- I scheduled pediatrician appointments, school visits, and other critical home-life obligations far in advance for the sake of planning and did everything I could not to let work eruptions force me to rearrange them.

But there were still plenty of things to test me. Like the time I was sitting in our pediatrician's office waiting while my daughter was getting a few routine inoculations. My Black-Berry rang, and I could see the caller ID letters "Trump National Golf Club" in the little window. It was my secretary, advising me that Donald Trump was on the line. The matter was very important. Just then the doctor came out of his office with my daughter in tow and began talking to me.

It didn't take more than a split second to make my decision. I simply said to my secretary, "Tell Mr. Trump I'm at the doctor's office and I will call him back!" and hung up.

(I did get back to you, Donald, and you can rest assured I took care of whatever it was—just in working mother's time!)

CAROLYN 101:

When it comes to kids and work, know where to draw the line; your kids *always* come first.

One day in the spring of 2002, Donald Trump came up to Trump National to play golf. When he mentioned that Mark Burnett, the creator of the hit reality show *Survivor*, had asked him to collaborate on a business-oriented reality show called *The Apprentice*, he asked me what I thought of the idea.

With visions of hordes of eager young people running around the upper floors of Trump Tower, or for that matter the workplaces of all the other Trump projects, including my own, my first reaction was that it would be too disruptive.

Being the let's-not-beat-around-the-bush type, I said, "It sounds pretty hokey."

In response, he just chuckled mysteriously.

As he always does, Donald listened calmly and carefully to my reaction. And then, like every good manager must sometimes do, he made an executive decision to ignore it. I had no idea at the time, of course, that I would have anything to do with this project. And even when I found out that I would be involved, I had not an inkling that this particular task would test everything I had learned about work-life balance to the limit, and beyond.

SIX

The Woman in the Workplace

To: Carolyn Kepcher [E-mail]

Forget the hoopla, you are a first-rate professional. And your digs on the women are right on. That dress and behavior would never be tolerated in any serious business situation (that's spoken by a lifetime female IBMer!). What does that sort of conduct say about society's respect for women, or more importantly, women's respect for themselves? I'm glad that you dumped on them for it. I've got a 34-year-old professional career daughter who was appalled at the way they dressed.

The War of the Sexes

By the filming of the third episode of *The Apprentice*, two of the original sixteen contestants had been fired. Both of the dismissed contestants had been men. The fourteen young contenders still standing remained divided into two sexually segregated teams: Protégé, staffed by eight women, and Versacorp, with six men. I remember that the theme of the episode was negotiation. The task assigned by the producers was to purchase items from a long list of commodities ranging from the prosaic (Peking duck and raw squid from Chinatown) to the glamorous (an ounce of gold from New York's Diamond District). At the end of the day, the team that had succeeded in negotiating the deepest discounts off retail price of the items would take the task. And the losing team would lose another one of its members.

My own task was one that I had accepted with some trepidation ten days before, when Donald Trump asked me to join him on his new show, along with The Trump Organization senior adviser George Ross. He wanted us to serve as his eyes and ears when the teams were out in the field and then join him in the boardroom to help determine who should be fired. Our involvement in the show would take only a few hours a week, he told us.

But I had quickly come to realize that estimate was not at all accurate! Especially at the end of this long, exhausting day of filming Episode 3, which had involved leaping out of a yellow cab that reeked of raw squid and dead duck to go dashing after the men of Versacorp down a crowded street in New York's Diamond District in my business suit and heels. Now all fourteen contestants and the tribunal of judges—Donald Trump, George Ross, and I—convened in the boardroom for Task Resolution. As we had at the close of the previous two episodes, George and I took turns presenting the bottom line to our CEO. Neither team had lost in money objective, bottom-line terms. But—and this was a big but—while the men of Versacorp had managed to negotiate a total of 9 percent off the full purchase price of the items, the women of Protégé had slashed the aggregate price of the items by a whopping 22 percent.

After being advised of this 13-percentage-point differential between the sexes, Donald Trump glared at the six remaining men before throwing up his hands. "I'm starting to think," he exclaimed, "that I'm never going to hire a man again!" From the way he said it, it wasn't immediately apparent that he was joking.

As a woman—particularly a woman who worked for Donald Trump—I should have been applauding that sentiment, right?

Wrong.

As a woman, I should have been proud of the women's unbroken string of victories, right?

Wrong.

As a woman, a working woman, and a corporate executive who has risen to a fairly high place in both an organization largely dominated by men (Trump) and an industry dominated by men (golf), I felt troubled and ashamed by the dubious means by which the women of Protégé were racking up their string of victories. By the fourth episode, when Protégé won yet again, the little slack I had been willing to cut the women for what appeared to have begun as an amusing gimmick was gone. Frankly, I was appalled.

The reason for my discomfort was simple: The women of Protégé, with batting eyes wide open, were using their sexuality to manipulate sales.

Victory, at What Cost?

At the beginning of Episode 1, the sixteen male and female contestants had been divided into all-men and all-women teams. To be fair to both sides of what would shortly blossom into a full-blown cultural controversy, this initial decision about team composition was the producers', not the contestants'. The battle of the sexes that ensued had made for some riveting television.

From the first moments of airtime, it became obvious to viewers that the interactions within the teams were breaking down according to commonly held sexual stereotypes. The men fraternized in a casual fashion that resembled the politics of the locker room or a football team. But the women, who at first bonded at least as solidly as the men, much more quickly experienced internal tensions that occasionally erupted into virulent disputes that some classified as "catfighting." (I should mention that George, Donald, and I were never permitted by the producers to review footage shot at the suite or the on-the-fly interviews. All of that material was kept under wraps until the nights the shows aired.)

Each team, after electing a project manager, was asked to go back to business basics. For example, the first assigned task was to pick a suitable location and sell lemonade. Both teams made some strategic mistakes as well as some good choices. Both teams suffered from organizational and logistical difficulties, internal dissent, breakdowns in the chain of command, and tactical errors. But both teams also persevered to the end, kept themselves together, and ultimately passed the test with flying colors—that is, both teams made money.

The men's team, which I was keeping tabs on, selected a poor location: at the South Street Seaport in lower Manhattan, within smelling distance of the Fulton Fish Market. But they had rebounded by the afternoon and, after hitting their stride, had doubled their $250 seed money into a perfectly respectable $500 pot. Particularly because they were achieved within an eight-hour period, their results were nothing to sneeze at.

The men had been feeling pretty good going into Task Resolution, until George, who had been monitoring the women, revealed that they had more than *quadrupled* their money. The men were shocked.

Only after I saw the tape of the women's selling scenes did I realize how they had pulled off their performance. The two teams had been running roughly neck and neck until some point in the midafternoon when, in response to the anxiety produced by an apparent sales slump, the women of Protégé had desperately started to rummage deeper into their kit bag of available resources. I could hardly object to that, since one should continually assess available resources while undertaking any task.

CAROLYN 101:
Not all resources are good ones.

Without (or so it seemed) giving the long-term ramifications of their tactics much thought, one of the female contestants had spontaneously started offering to kiss male customers in exchange for purchasing lemonade at the staggering price of five dollars a cup. Needless to say, since the contestant was young and attractive, she found no shortage of takers. And since nothing in life succeeds like success, one of the other women began handing out her phone number to gawking male purchasers, which also boosted the going price of a cup of lemonade from Protégé to premium levels.

As a judge—even though I had not been the one who followed Protégé—I had some good things and bad things to say about this conduct. On the plus side:

- They had distinguished themselves from their competitors.
- They had utilized available resources.
- They had made an accurate assessment of the interests of their customers.
- They had succeeded in the essence of branding, which is to raise the *apparent* value of a product by endowing it with glamour and appeal.
- They were having fun.

On the negative side, I made another list:

- They had exposed themselves to possible criticism as being manipulative.

- They had reinforced unpleasant and unproductive sexual stereotypes.
- Although they had successfully created a brand image—Sexy Lemonade—they had simultaneously damaged their brand value by undermining its core credibility.
- They had forsaken building long-term value in exchange for short-term gain.

We as their judges had not gone out of our way to explain that we might have criteria other than financial success on which to judge their performance. We had never openly discussed whether we were planning, in effect, to deduct points on some invisible merit scoreboard based on intangible issues such as comportment and personal presentation.

However, we had every reason to expect that they would get the message that it wasn't always just "Money wins." Donald Trump had been perfectly frank in his opening statement to the contestants: "This is not a game. It's a thirteen-week job interview." As you learned in Chapter 4, the way one conducts oneself during a job interview, the way one manages one's personal presentation, whether one projects an image of honesty and sobriety or irresponsibility and laxness, are all critical factors in determining any employer's final decision on one's value as a prospective employee.

The bottom line: They should have anticipated how all of this was going to go over.

CAROLYN 101:

**Image isn't everything, and if you've got it,
it doesn't always pay to flaunt it.**

Coffee, Tea, or Me?

I wasn't inclined to take a terribly hard line with the women over the lemonade incident. I was inclined to cut them some slack based on the following grounds:

- The women of Protégé were not representing me or The Trump Organization—they were representing themselves.
- Their sales strategies seemed to have developed in a lighthearted, spontaneous way.
- They had gotten creative about their strategic assets and had achieved an incredible bottom line.

Then came the second episode. This task was considerably more complicated and required a more sophisticated set of business skills. Both teams were asked to prepare full-blown advertising campaigns for the premium flight services of Marquis Jet, a fractional-ownership private jet company in which the famed investor Warren Buffet is a major stockholder.

Both teams were technically working for the prominent

New York advertising man Donny Deutsch, a good friend of Donald Trump's who had founded his own ad company and recently sold it to a large conglomerate for $300 million. Both teams met with Donny, but the project manager for Versacorp, Jason Curtis, committed a vital strategic error by failing to hold a meeting with the client on the spurious grounds that there wasn't enough time. In the advertising business, there is always time to meet with the client.

Further, in conceiving of their product, the women blatantly relied on sexual symbolism. They turned the jet's nose into a phallic symbol to sell the glamour of fractional jet ownership. In their favor, this approach was somewhat more sophisticated than a straightforward "sex sells" campaign. The imagery and artwork were assembled with irony and a certain amount of taste. I'd call the approach playfully naughty rather than indecent, and on the whole it was a slick, professional job.

I felt okay about this win, too, because of Protégé's wise strategic decision to meet with the clients. So, while I may not have wholly approved of their campaign—I believed that Protégé's win was a fair victory.

Dress for Success

To the pitch meeting with the client, also attended by Donny Deutsch, the women of Protégé had decided to add to the appeal of their pitch by wearing costumes meant to evoke the sexy stewardesses of the golden age of pre-regulation aviation.

Although I thought the costumes were a rookie decision, the technique was amusing, effective, and, in that particular context, not inappropriate, because the advertising business is one in which a broad interpretation of the meaning of "business attire" is not merely permitted, but actively encouraged.

The women of Protégé's choice of attire on a number of other occasions certainly raised eyebrows, from audience members as well as my own. I probably received more e-mail on this particular topic than any other during the period in which *The Apprentice* aired. Nearly all of the remarks and comments, most of them scathing and few approving, seemed to suggest that the women were crossing some sort of ill-defined line of propriety when they dressed in ways which, to put it mildly, drew attention to their natural charms.

Using myself as an example, I will admit that I also came in for my share of criticism during the show for dressing too conservatively, in permanent executive mode. Let me provide you with a peek into my thought process as I selected my wardrobe. For the boardroom scenes, in which George Ross and I figured most prominently, I very deliberately selected my attire with a simple goal in mind: I wanted candidates and viewers to take me seriously. I also knew that the boardroom scenes were serious, somber, and sober in tone, and I attempted to reflect that atmosphere with my attire. I also knew that I was going to be appearing on national television not merely representing myself, but The Trump Organization and Trump National Golf Clubs as well.

Bearing that goal in mind, and keeping in mind that I

couldn't err on the side of being too conservative—or so I thought—it was about halfway through the airing of the first season's episodes when an attractive young woman came up to me in a restaurant.

"Carolyn," she said, "I just want you to know how profound an influence you've had on me. Like you, I want to be taken seriously at work, so I make sure to keep my hair up at work, I never wear any makeup, and I dress very conservatively so that no one will think that I'm using my looks to get ahead. I consider you my role model in this area."

My instantaneous reaction was to say, "You know, I think you've got it all wrong." I felt terrible that this good-looking young woman had interpreted my sartorial choices as somehow suggesting that it is inappropriate for a young woman to dress attractively in the workplace. We all know how in the early eighties, businesswomen were encouraged to wear wide-shouldered power suits and to dress, in effect, just like men. And we all know that in the nineties, a backlash to that puritanical and asexual trend ensued, which has resulted in a certain degree of confusion and ambiguity as to what is appropriate attire in the workplace.

Let me, if I may, share some of my thoughts on the subject with you. In every case, I believe that the primary questions you have to ask yourself are:

- What am I trying to accomplish in this situation, both long-term and short-term?
- Who or what am I representing? Myself? My organization? My industry? My nation? My gender?

In most professional situations, particularly if you are young and female, it usually is a higher-risk move to dress provocatively than it is to dress conservatively. In a business context, the primary goal is typically to come across as business-like and serious. But as with everything else, moderation is the goal. I dress much more casually when I'm around the golf course meeting the members than I do when meeting with clients in midtown Manhattan or even with clients at the club.

Not long ago I interviewed an attractive young woman for a job with our organization. We had not specified in the help-wanted ad whether the person she was interviewing with—me—was a man or a woman. She came in wearing a very short skirt and a very low-cut top, and right away I knew what she was up to. The interview was unexceptional, and, on her way out, she looked down at herself, looked up at me, and said with a shy smile, "I guess I thought I was going to be interviewed by a man."

"I know you thought that." I smiled back at her, and that was all that we needed to say.

To young women in business just starting out, my advice is very basic. Save your money, and rather than spending it on all sorts of elegant work outfits, I would buy two good-quality suits, possibly one with a not-too-short skirt and one with pants, to be worn with a blouse that is not too low cut. The key word being "too." Not *too* casual. Not *too* corporate. Not *too* stiff. Not *too* loose. It is all about appropiateness.

You get the picture, and you get the clothes. The goal here is to wear something that doesn't call too much attention to itself. We should be looking at you, not what you're wearing.

Winning Isn't Everything

During the third episode, reviewing the videotape of the women's negotiating sessions, I began to be affronted by their behavior. The "sex sells" approach had become a habit. There were a number of antics that I could neither condone or approve. Here are two examples:

- One woman, bargaining for a food item with a male counterman, lifted her skimpy top and exposed her belly. She rubbed her stomach provocatively, whimpered something about how hungry she was, and asked whether *he* could see how hungry she was.
- All the women giggled as they pleaded with a bemused gold dealer to provide them a discount. When he refused, they jumped up and down, begging, "Please, please!" in girlish voices and batting their eyelashes.

The women of Protégé were not displaying good negotiating skills. Begging, pleading, acting provocative, and flirting are not negotiating. They are seduction. Negotiations in which one party feels unfairly manipulated do not tend to end well for either side.

And as a business method, this "negotiation" seemed utterly lacking in creativity. These bright, experienced women—including a political consultant, an account executive, a stockbroker, a marketing manager—not only were not thinking outside the box, but weren't even thinking. They were falling into a rut.

It was entirely to their credit that these were engaging and attractive women. And I wouldn't have been at all surprised if at various times in their careers they had used their physical attraction to get ahead—a little. They were young and vivacious. But they were also *already* successful in business. Had they achieved their success by wiggling their midriffs and batting their eyelashes?

I'd seen it coming, by the way, in my first visit to the set of *The Apprentice* on the fourth floor of Trump Tower. We met all the contestants in the boardroom, and some of the women—not all—when they introduced themselves to Donald, threw their hair and swiveled to meet his eyes as if they were trying to pick him up at the bar at Cipriani's. It wasn't a big deal in and of itself, but I noted it and chalked it up to people's common perception of Donald Trump based on headlines about his romantic life.

But by the end of the third episode, I was officially feeling put off by the women's approach. I didn't like the fact that no one was saying a word about this pattern. For years male-dominated corporations have successfully defended themselves from charges of sexual discrimination and even harassment by claiming, in effect, that if women acted provocatively, they somehow "deserved" it. This is of course nonsense to us now. But in some ways we still have a long way to go. The general behavior of the women of Protégé struck me as setting back the image of women in the workplace.

By the time we got to the fourth episode, I was keeping my eye on the women as well as the men. Both teams were asked to manage the Times Square branch of Planet Hollywood for one night. The winning team would be the one that took in the highest revenues in three areas: bar sales, food sales, and merchandise sales. Once again, men and women were pitted against each other. And once again, the women seemed to feel as if being super-sexy made them virtually untouchable. They weren't being businesswomen.

Early in the planning process, the women made a joint decision to imitate the sexually charged style of the restaurant chain Hooters. They came up with a concept they called "Shooters," in reference to downing shots of booze at a bar. Dressed in a variety of styles that fit the "Shooters" theme, including tight halter tops and hip-hugging jeans, they started selling shots on the floor, carrying the shot glasses on trays, which gave them a golden opportunity to display their bare midriffs to an appreciative, mostly male clientele. As the manager of Planet Hollywood—and we, the judges—looked on in mounting concern, some of the women began drinking with the customers and, at one point, selling alcohol to a man who clearly had had way too much to drink already.

The Planet Hollywood manager felt compelled to take the women aside. He reminded them that they were exposing him personally and his restaurant to a possible lawsuit for serving liquor to a customer who was already intoxicated. Furthermore, the women had broken rules and regulations against service staff drinking with customers on the job.

That's when I decided the women of Protégé had crossed

the line. They were no longer representing themselves. They were representing Planet Hollywood, a major international brand. They were also, although less directly, representing The Trump Organization, where they all one day aspired to work. And that, in a nutshell, was their real problem. They had gotten so caught up in winning that they forgot that *how* you win counts when a future boss is watching.

CAROLYN 101:

Winning isn't everything. *How* you win counts just as much.

Taking a Stand

The morning after Planet Hollywood, I walked into Donald Trump's office and laid my cards on the table. "This is getting out of hand," I said, and I expected he had felt the same.

He hesitated for just a moment and shrugged. Then he said, "You know, you're right."

I felt compelled to go to him because by this point I believed we were, in effect, handing out rewards for victories that had been attained by less than legitimate means. As a senior female executive at The Trump Organization, I was acutely sensitive to the importance of correcting any possible perception that we were in favor of such behavior.

There was also a personal factor to be considered: the reward the women of Protégé had won for their victory at Planet Hollywood was an afternoon of sun, golf, and fun at the Trump National Golf Club. And while I had no doubt that this was the sort of recreation they could sorely benefit from, following their antics of the previous evening, it didn't sit well with me to stage a celebration at our golf course in honor of a victory won by methods of which I couldn't approve. They hadn't broken any overt rules; they had simply failed to recognize the long-term consequences of their behavior.

The decision to, in effect, engineer a behavior course correction for the women of Protégé was then made in true Trump Organization fashion. As Donald Trump's manager, I had isolated the problem. I had brought it to his attention—although he would have had to have been blind to have missed it, and he was certainly not blind, particularly to the provocative behavior of beautiful women. But without delay, we were going to fix it. "Since we're going up to the golf club this afternoon," he said, "let's do it there."

This series of incidents had reinforced for me why most if not all corporations these days have ethics and morals codes on the books—employees and managers need to know that there are boundaries and limits.

Here were women who had worked at, among other institutions, Merrill Lynch, Clinique, and the Clinton White House (okay, don't laugh) or had founded their own successful businesses. I'd seen it happen before in the vicinity of Donald Trump and The Trump Organization—they may have been blinded by the glamour and the glitz, the remarkable settings and lifestyle, and become immune to the long-term implications of their conduct. They may have just wanted to win, no holds barred. Well, we needed to tell them that some holds need to be barred.

We agreed to handle the issue as sensitively and intelligently as possible. Mr. Trump and I invited all the team members to my office at the club. I began by saying that I completely understood how it had happened. "You just wanted to win the game," I said sympathetically. "Who doesn't?" But I explained that this was not just a battle of dollars and cents, it was also a battle of image and perceptions. And that it was vitally important that people not get the impression that the women were advancing toward their goal of landing a $250,000 job as the president of a division of The Trump Organization by using sex to sell.

This entire process, I reminded them, had been designed for us to get to know them, both individually and as a group. Did they really want us to remember that they won a task because they hiked up their skirts? They were risking losing out on being candidates with a reputation that befit a Donald Trump apprentice.

Then Donald said his piece: "You are smart, dynamic, and attractive women. You beat the guys fair and square. But you're coming a little close to crossing the line. Relying on your sexuality to win. Well, it's unnecessary."

This wasn't behavior or comportment, I added, befitting a future president of one of Donald Trump's companies.

The women looked a bit chastised and embarrassed, as indeed they should have been. And I felt proud of Donald Trump's willingness to put his foot down on the right side of this question, wanting to play the mentor and to show them that they didn't need to stoop to manipulative techniques to win.

There are plenty of male bosses out there who might have been inclined to encourage this behavior or at least not actively discourage it. I was also impressed that Donald had trusted my judgment, and had—once again—supported me.

At precisely this point in the show, with four men down and four standing, the men and women were mixed on new teams. After that, two curious things happened. The catfighting among the women stopped. And while the women, no longer egged on by one another, didn't entirely curtail their use of sexual weaponry as a competitive edge—they did stop using it as a prop and began relying more on their brains instead.

The Making of Carolyn

Also at this point, somewhat inadvertently, I found myself stepping into the spotlight of controversy. Every day now my e-mail in-box was flooded. At first I was taken aback by the intensity of the public's response to the stance we took. Clearly, without intending to, we had touched a sensitive cultural nerve. Throughout the tapings, I had come to know and admire Mark Burnett, the elegant, witty, exceedingly sharp British producer of not just *The Apprentice* but other hit reality shows. He had an interesting take on this issue: "The reason the public is reacting to you so strongly is that while they are forced to sit silently by, you actually get to express what they are feeling. So you are the spokeswoman for the public. And what they see in you is a woman who is precisely the opposite of the women of Protégé, a woman who succeeded without having to compromise but who is also not hiding her natural attractions under a loose-fitting outfit."

I suppose I agree. When people accuse me of coming off a little stiff or uptight in my attire on the show, I typically ask them, "How would you propose to dress for a business meeting or a board meeting?"

The fact that we had chosen to take this stand on behalf of maintaining a positive image of women in the workplace made us spokespeople on the issue. I even appeared on several talk shows to discuss the topic with leaders in business studies. The public turned our program into a national referendum on women in the workplace. I believe this was one of the primary reasons that the show became so popular. Of course, the sexual politics made for terrific television. But as our appearances on this and countless other media outlets demonstrated, we had succeeded in dramatizing in a serious—and, yes, realistic—way the fact that gender differences and similarities continue to enliven and bedevil society.

I will mention just one media moment I experienced during this limelight period, which may shed some additional light on this hot-button issue. When I appeared on the daytime TV show *The View*, the cohost Meredith Vieira commented, "You seem to dress in a very business-like manner on the show." Before I could even respond, the comedienne Joy Behar cut in:

"Well, I don't think Donald Trump would have minded one bit if you'd worn a bikini to work!"

Not only was this an insultingly inaccurate summation of the role of women at The Trump Organization—not to mention my personal style of dress—but it was a wildly inaccurate description of the current position of women in the workplace, and *The View* is a show a lot of people watch. Needless to say, it was not a joke that I found funny.

Still feeling steamed about it later that day, I was answering some e-mail when the following came in:

To: Carolyn Kepcher [E-mail]

Dear Ms. Kepcher:

I just wanted to thank you for being such a positive role model for women. I must admit that prior to *The Apprentice* I had no idea who you were. As I continued to watch, I found myself more intrigued with you than with the contestants, especially after you took the women to task for using their sexuality as a means to win the weekly challenge.

I just watched *The View* today and noticed that you became somewhat upset when Joy commented that your success had come from your looks. While I don't doubt that Mr. Trump does see that you are an incredibly beautiful woman, I highly doubt that he would be willing to entrust a multimillion-dollar company to someone based solely on their looks.

For what it's worth, I just wanted to let you know that not

everyone out there thinks that your accomplishments have come as a result of good genes. There are some of us, hopefully many of us, who see beyond that. Keep up the good work, Anna

Thank you for those e-mails, because sometimes they are just what I need to get through a long day at the office.

SEVEN

The Good Team

To: Carolyn Kepcher [E-mail]

It has been a pleasure to watch you these past months on *The Apprentice.* You are what is right with business in America today. I applauded your evaluations of the various contestants, agreed with your dismissal of the women's usage of sex appeal to manipulate sales, and learned a great deal from you regarding how any business person should present and conduct themselves in a professional environment.

Do you give or have you considered giving seminars on succeeding in business to MBA candidates across the country? More specifically, could you share any advice with us regarding how you seem to interact so well with other people on the job and as a leader? I am thinking about how you manage all the challenges of running a top-flight organization. How do you forge a winning team?

Team Trump

I had to spend a great deal of time out of the office while shooting the first season of *The Apprentice*. This required developing a certain degree of flexibility in communicating with my staff by phone and by BlackBerry. It also required my staff once again to prove themselves as a team. There's no greater test of a good team in action than when it plays without its boss. On my first day back at work, I couldn't have felt prouder of the fact that Confucius, the sage of order, as opposed to the gremlins of chaos and confusion, had clearly reigned in my absence. I certainly did not feel threatened by the fact that, all things considered, events had proceeded smoothly without me. If anything, I saw it more as a sign that I have taught my team well and that many of my colleagues and I have now been working together harmoniously for a number of years. In this, I have emulated Donald Trump's preference for training people and providing them with sufficient rewards to maintain one of the lowest turnover rates in the industry.

CAROLYN 101:

The best team is the team that continues
to perform even when the manager is absent.

This style of working together might be described as "collegial," although "orchestral" also captures some of the feel. The word "collegial" has the same root as "colleague," and being collegial means sharing an understanding that decisions of importance should be discussed in an environment of openness, honesty, courtesy, and clarity. Being collegial does not mean that we do not have a strict chain of command, nor that we do not defer to authority. What it does mean is that to every extent possible we govern our operations according to a philosophy of—to use another term drawn from academia—peer-to-peer review. Perhaps the simplest way to describe this style of operating is "leading by example." I try as much as I can to *show* (as opposed to *tell*) my colleagues how to work best *with* other people instead of *for* them.

What I Learned About Teams from My Family

At a number of points in my still fairly short life, I have been fortunate to play on winning teams, in some cases as team leader. Whenever I have thought about building a new team, I've tried to model on the strengths of the winning teams from my past.

The first team that most of us play on is our family, and that first team has an enormous effect on our personal development. With all the talk today about dysfunctional families, we know that many family teams are not destined to win gold medals in the domestic Olympics. But my siblings and I were fortunate to have been raised in a family that functioned very effectively as a team, and we attribute our current success to the competent management of our two cocaptains, our parents.

I trace my healthy, evolved view of the gender dynamic in the workplace back to my parents, who were equal, mutually supportive players and partners in life. I never knew them to rely on gender characteristics—feminine wiles, masculine strength—to achieve dominance over each other. I grew up never doubting that it is not only possible but desirable for men and women to cooperate and collaborate, not to compete on the basis of traditional sexual roles. My father never expressed the slightest resentment of my mother's professional success, even when there were some years that she made more money than he did. My mother, for her part, never felt that it was appropriate to rely solely on my father for leadership, guidance, and support.

I also credit my family with my strong work ethic. My first work experience began at age twelve, when I sold Avon products that my mother would obtain from the Avon head office. She was the official Avon representative, but my sisters and I did the selling. Not door to door but to the women who worked at the New Rochelle City Hall, where my father worked. I didn't get to keep the money I earned; I turned it over to my mother to spend on us as she saw fit. So from that early age I was intimately familiar with the value of a dollar, and it has been an intimate relationship ever since. (My son, Connor, seems to be picking this up even earlier: While we were eyeing some live lobster floating in a tank at our local supermarket, he asked if we could buy some. I explained that lobster is very expensive. Some time later, Connor was asked if he knew what money is for. "To buy lobster!" he confidently replied.)

What I Learned About Teams
from Playing Sports

Some of the business strategies I use today I learned on a volleyball court. Really! When I won an academic scholarship to a prestigious high school, I stumbled across another winning team. One day after school, when just about every other girl either had gone home or was involved in some extracurricular activity, I was stuck waiting for my mother to pick me up. I was feeling a little sorry for myself, wondering whether it was worth it to start tackling my homework, when I heard cheers and shouts coming from the gym. I wandered in and came across a volleyball practice in full swing. One of the girls caught sight of me and shouted out, from deep within the goodness of her heart, "Hey, want to join in?"

I'd never played volleyball in my life. But the thrill of being asked easily overcame any apprehension I had about my lack of skill. Every time one of us failed to get the ball over the net, she had to run a lap. And in the beginning I ran so many laps that practice felt more like a marathon. But something made me want to stick it out and get better. I knew what it was: that older girl's voice, shouting out that she was willing to take a chance on the new girl, based on nothing but a moment's glance.

CAROLYN 101:

Self-confidence begins with your teammates demonstrating confidence in you.

I learned a great deal about self-confidence and drive during that phase of my life. I learned, for one thing, that if you are properly motivated, there are very few limits to your achievement. My motivation to succeed was rooted, I believe, in the immense satisfaction we all received from winning as a highly functional team. And the sport that we played is, as you can no doubt imagine, a different pastime from what you see at the beach. It takes timing and strength, skill, strategy, and finesse. Volleyball is cooperative, collaborative, fluid, and spontaneous. It takes a team working together, not some collection of high-profile stars showing off simply to win or, even worse, winning simply to show off. In volleyball, individual achievement *is* group achievement. No one person, no matter how talented, can carry the field.

CAROLYN 101:

Individual achievement is group achievement.

As in every collaborative enterprise, whether it's on the court or in an office, the major task of the captains and coaches is to figure out which player does what best. I fairly quickly emerged, with the encouragement of one of our coaches—both college students and great motivators—as a good outside hitter. This meant that my strong suit was going for the power hit, a shot usually taken from somewhere toward the front of the court. Being a good outside hitter required more than physical strength and agility. It required a mastery of strategy.

CAROLYN 101:

**Strategy is all about identifying an advantage
or opportunity before your opponent does,
and then seizing it quickly.**

I learned when and how to spot an empty patch on the other side of the court, and to make very sure that my opponent didn't figure it out before I could drop the ball into it. Through this fakery, I could, at least half the time, penetrate our opponents' defenses, but I did need the cover of a sharp team to deliver. Throwing an opponent off the scent is a skill that has come in handy countless times in my business career, but it is the importance of team backup that has really stuck with me.

By the time I graduated from high school, I was the volleyball captain. During my junior and senior years, we pulled off both undefeated seasons and state championships. When I arrived at the school, the glass trophy cases in the front hall had held some old, dusty awards. But with the help of our coaches and a superbly unified team, we took home enough trophies and championships to fill it and earn me, as captain, a full college scholarship, which at the time felt not unlike winning a job with The Trump Organization, the best team I've ever worked on.

Meeting of the Minds

One of the most revealing situations in which to gauge the effectiveness of a business team is a meeting. It's no surprise that many people who work in offices question the effectiveness of meetings. One of the most common complaints I hear from my fellow professionals is that meetings seem to drag on aimlessly and feel like a huge waste of time. Well, let's just say that time is of the essence in our meetings at Trump. And even though some believe that, in an age of e-mail, fax, cell phones, and collaborative enterprise software, meetings have become anachronisms, I don't agree—team face time is essential.

CAROLYN 101:
The true purpose and value of a meeting is to hone and practice a winning strategy.

In our organization, all meetings have three goals:

1. To create solidarity of purpose and a sense of being on a shared mission. That much of the information exchanged at a meeting could arguably be captured in memos and sent by group e-mails is not, in my opinion, the point. For the sake of the team, electronic communications should supplement instead of supplant face-to-face interaction whenever possible.
2. To share information in such a way that it reinforces the process of solving problems collectively, as opposed to individually or even in one-to-one meetings between employee and manager. This all goes back to the adage that "two heads are better than one," and excellent innovations can be hatched in an exchange among team members, benefiting from their collective wisdom.
3. To expose any looming internal problems or confusion so they can be straightened out before they become genuine threats to the team's effectiveness.

We don't generally post our internal governance rules, but if I were obliged to do so, I would hang the following "Rules of the Meeting" on the wall of our conference room. In real life, my colleagues have learned these rules on the job.

1. All meetings are conducted according to the One-Minute Rule. If I call a meeting for 10:00, by 10:01 I close the door. Anyone who turns up later misses the

meeting. (Since the institution of this rule, our attendance record has been 100 percent.)

2. We always have an agenda. I always prepare the agenda.
3. We all understand that we will likely be covering topics not mentioned on the agenda. But we also understand that we will address those topics only once all the items on the agenda have been covered.
4. We encourage input from all participants. That said, we never let meetings be dominated by one or two voices. We tend to give extra weight to the experts in their fields, the department heads.
5. Before speaking, we ask ourselves these questions:
   - *Does this input truly contribute to our general understanding of the issue? (With the unspoken question being, Am I just showing off?)*
   - *Am I providing a fresh perspective, or could I be undermining the authority of the person to whom I am directing my suggestions?*

At the first staff meeting I called following my return from the TV shoot, one of my department heads decided to be a little too generous with his comments on a wide variety of topics, most if not all tangential to his fields of knowledge. As manager, I had a few options for responding to him. The speaker didn't seem to appreciate that the department head he was criticizing—or "informing"—was becoming upset by the sharpness of his "advice." The easiest approach would have been to advise the department head, in the presence of the other staff members, to remember Rule 5.

I chose not to exercise that option, though, in part because I wanted him to be able to save face. But I also knew that I had to tread a fine line between stifling ideas that, given their lack of expertise, might provide a fresh take on a subject and wasting everybody's time with hot air. I decided to hold two separate private meetings *immediately* after the staff meeting. I stress *immediately* because:

CAROLYN 101:

Problems within a team dynamic are like a cancer:
You have to remove them before
they spread throughout the system.

Having identified a source of disharmony, I knew I had to nip it in the bud. I began my one-on-one meeting with the long-winded team member as I always do, by stressing the positive. "I appreciate your input," I said, making a point to praise one idea he had tossed out, which I thought might have some merit. "But I think your feedback would be better received if you made sure to speak mainly to subjects that you are better prepared to address."

I asked my colleague (very gently) to try to think before he spoke about how his questions and comments would likely be received. How did he want to come off to his colleagues? As a busybody? As hypercritical? As ignorant? As supportive? It wasn't, I assured him, that I didn't want him to speak up. I merely wanted him to do so with a clearly defined purpose.

One reason we had these staff meetings was to catch minor problems before they became major problems. For all I knew, what seemed like a case of one person dominating a single meeting might—if not corrected—have developed into a serious rivalry between two department heads. What the meeting had uncovered, fortunately, was that at least two of my colleagues weren't communicating effectively. My colleague seemed to appreciate the way I discussed the situation. He took the criticism in stride, and I ended up being impressed by his response. That was a win-win.

I then called a meeting with the department head who had been the target of our colleague's suggestions. Again I began with a positive, then got down to the heart of the matter. "What I didn't hear from you today was any active or constructive response to your colleague's suggestions." I had to let this department head know that she needed to be more proactive in maintaining authority over her area of expertise by giving her evaluation of the thoughts being proffered. She also needed to accept that even if the advice had been delivered in a manner that was not very sensitive, that there was something to what he was saying. Where there's smoke, there's fire.

Faultfinding, Finger-Pointing, Tattletaling

One of the most potent threats to the cohesion of a team occurs when one staff member points a faultfinding finger at another. The criticism may be delivered behind the target's back—in some cases, appropriately so—directly to the person's face, or through rumor or innuendo.

Obviously, my reactions to these criticisms tend to be determined by my perception of the critic's motivation. If it is:

- Well intentioned
- Justified and accurate
- Delivered for the good of the team

I applaud it. But if it is, or seems to be:

- Self-aggrandizing
- Undermining
- Mean-spirited

I do everything I can to take the criticizer down a notch. I recently had occasion to say (sharply) to an employee whose criticism seemed to fit in the latter category, "I didn't ask you to point fingers. But I do need to determine who is responsible for this breakdown so that we can move quickly to fix it."

The opposite side of this equation, of course, is when employees cover one another's backsides. And I have to admit, I've got a bit of a soft spot on that one. In my experience, that is what good team members do, and on the whole, it facilitates bonding. If it's one friend covering for another, I fully expect that favor to be returned. That's part of all of us wanting us to succeed. Such instinctive cooperation and collaboration is why good teams work so well.

CAROLYN 101:

"Cover for me" isn't a sign of weakness in a team, it's a sign of strength.

Except, of course, when people cover for each other in such a way that disguises a weakness that needs to be addressed— lying, for example, or cheating for another.

If there is any ambiguity about responsibility, I do expect the employee to own up to his or her mistake, take the consequences in stride, and move on.

When Employees Collide

Sometimes, employees just don't get along. And sometimes that's obvious. As a student of human nature, I sympathize, but as a team coach, I have no patience for personal vendettas that impede team performance. I expect all my team members to cooperate and collaborate, and if mutual antipathy gets in the way—or is even perceived to be getting in the way, which is nearly as bad—I will not hesitate to call it as I see it, even if that means sitting both team members down to work through it face-to-face with my facilitation. I just won't tolerate active disharmony in a team. If I can't fix it any other way, either one or both of those employees will have to go. Not liking someone is just human nature, but failing to work for the common goal is bad for business.

When Employees Get Too Close for Comfort

Every once in a while, relationships form among team members that interfere with the cohesion of the whole in a completely different way. Romantic relationships, or even close friendships, can sometimes have an impact that isn't necessarily desirable. What happens outside the office is none of my business, but if the balance of the team is thrown off, I will make it clear that an adjustment has to be made.

I'll give you two examples.

A number of years back, I learned the way we always learn of such things—through the grapevine—that one of my department heads, a man, appeared to be demonstrating favoritism toward one of his co-workers, a woman. No one was quite sure what was going on, but let's just say that it had become obvious to the staff that the department head was partial to her.

The problem was not whether they were having an affair. The problem was that other staff members had become convinced that because of his special relationship to her, that she was, for example, being excused from performing certain onerous duties that they all were supposed to share equally. Even more disruptively, certain other staff members in the department had become convinced that the only way to gain the approval of the chief was by befriending this woman due to the extraordinary influence she appeared to hold over him.

Clearly, I had to step in.

Calling him into my office, I told him two things.

"I am not interested in what is happening after work hours," I said. "But I do care about the perception that you have created, because perceptions, after all, are facts. The perception here is that you have been giving this woman an unfair advantage. I am not here to find out the truth, but I am here to tell you that this is creating a problem, which is that your behavior is adversely affecting the integrity of the team."

He had only two possible responses to this confrontation. He could deny everything and apologize, or he could admit everything and apologize. He chose to do the latter. He admitted that he had been partial to her. He didn't admit that there was any romance going on. I told him that as his manager, I considered it my job to call this situation to his attention, in case he hadn't been aware of its full ramifications. What happened next was up to him.

He now faced his own image problem. If he suddenly stopped demonstrating partiality to her, it would seem as if he had simply discarded her. But if he continued to show favoritism, he would obviously lose his own job. If he fired her, she would have every reason to reproach him for unfair treatment. He had to fix a perception, and once fixed in people's minds, perceptions are difficult things to change. What he did was to slowly disengage himself from her, but in such a way as to permit her to maintain her dignity. Whether they ever got together, or broke up, outside the workplace was not relevant. What stopped was the favoritism, and the unity of the whole was restored.

A similar situation occurred during the first season of *The Apprentice*, when Amy Henry and Nick Warnock appeared to be getting a little too close for comfort. Once again, whether a romance itself was flowering in the suite at Trump Tower was beside the point. What mattered was that when Amy, Nick, and Katrina lost a task at the Taj Mahal, Amy, as Project Manager, chose Katrina to accompany her to the boardroom. In the boardroom, when Donald Trump asked Katrina why she thought Amy had chosen her, as opposed to Nick, to share fault for the loss, Katrina speculated that she believed it was because Amy and Nick were involved in a "relationship." The nature of the relationship was, once again, immaterial. What mattered was that by getting involved with each other, Nick and Amy had collaborated in creating an impression of favoritism.

Expanding the Franchise

All of this emphasis on team building and performance at the Trump golf resorts is based on an informal philosophy of the Trump Organization. We go out of our way to help one another out on the assumption that if one of us succeeds, we all succeed. Recently, Andy Weiss, one of the VP's running our Chicago construction operations, was looking to close a major deal. He called me up to see if I might be able to host him and his clients for a round of golf. I am not generally in the habit of hosting nonmembers and their guests on the course, which is exclusively reserved for the members. But in the interest of teamwork for the greater good of the organization, Andy and I found a way to make it happen. We put together a wonderful outing delivered in the Trump style, and sure enough, the deal closed. "It's nothing personal, it's just business," you hear people say. But sometimes, when we're playing on the same team, it *is* personal—and that's just the way it should be.

As it was when I was shooting *The Apprentice*. Since I had to spend nearly all my time in and around midtown Manhattan during the course of the shooting, the New York office went out of its way to provide me with office space and whatever assistance I needed to take care of anything urgent. At one point during the shooting, I had to prepare a budget for the Bedminster property. Our very CFO, knowing we were on a tight deadline, provided me with the information I needed to get the job done quickly so quality would not be compromised. The team pride at Trump made this possible during a hectic time for me.

The Tag Teams of Reality TV

Although I have a "real" team at Trump National, the teams with which I have been most associated lately are the ones composed of candidates on *The Apprentice*. As every viewer knows, the theme of teamwork is never far from the dramatic thrust of the show. Whether it is a friendship springing up between Kwame and Troy, antipathy developing between Omarosa and Ereka, or the hint of romance between Amy and Nick, the show effectively showcased many of the dynamics that, on the one hand, glue teams together and, on the other, pull them apart.

Of the many examples of team behavior I observed on the show, one sticks in my mind as an example of teamwork at its best and its worst. This was during the negotiation skills episode of *The Apprentice*'s first season, when I found myself in the front seat of a taxi with three members of the all-male team, Versacorp, squeezed into the backseat.

The cameras rolled as I took some mental notes on the team breakdown that was occurring. In my opinion, the seeds of the disruption had been sown earlier that day. Within minutes of his election as project manager, Sam Solovey, an Internet executive, made his first strategic decision.

In an admirable if ultimately futile attempt to organize the team's time more efficiently, he had divided his cohorts into two cadres of three each and appointed one field team (composed of Bill Rancic, the ultimate winner of the first season; Kwame Jackson, a Harvard MBA and former investment manager at Goldman Sachs; and Bowie Hogg, a FedEx account executive) to go running around Manhattan negotiating for an assortment of items on a long laundry list. The other group was the headquarters team, to which he named himself; Nick Warnock, a Xerox salesman; and Troy McClain, a mortgage lender and real estate developer, to direct operations from a central location and, I might add, considerable comfort.

I firmly believe, by now on the basis of extensive personal experience, that poor Sam shot himself in the foot from the moment he made that decision. No team should be split so that one half sits in an ivory tower while the other is expected to get its hands dirty. He was leading blindly from the control room; a coach needs to be on the field.

CAROLYN 101:

**Give great thought to the situation and personalities
at hand before splitting a team.**

Sam had the interests of his team at heart. He decided that if he could get his field team to negotiate a significant discount off the price of an ounce of gold, the biggest ticket item on the list of items to be gathered, then the team could have an easier ride with the other items. But he had destroyed the value of that initiative by becoming fixated—there is no other word for it—on the prospect of his field team getting to the Diamond District before noon to buy the gold, under the assumption that they could get a better deal in the morning. As time ticked by, the members of Versacorp with me in that taxicab began to suspect that this was not an altogether solid plan.

"Drop everything you're doing and rush up to the Diamond District to get that gold immediately!" Sam shouted over his cell phone. "If you get there at any time after 11:30 A.M., the price is going to go up!"

At this point the team's resentment began to show. "The price of gold is just not going to change so quickly that time is the critical factor here!" Kwame said tersely yet calmly. His mildly defiant tone touched off a rebellion against Sam's leadership.

It dawned on the men that their team leader not only was not infallible but might well be completely out of his element. The scene that ensued was reminiscent of one of those old war movies in which a group of enlisted men refuse an officer's command to mount a futile charge into an opposing cannon.

"This guy's a nut," one of the other teammates remarked caustically. When not a soul in the cab spoke up in defense of their leader, I knew that Sam had lost control of his team by not acknowledging Kwame's tone and allowing him to air any grievances or share his opinion. By ordering them around, Sam had made it clear to the team that they had no voice.

CAROLYN 101:

**All team members must feel that they have a voice
that will be heard by their teammates.**

But then something unexpected took place that reinforced the mysterious power of teams to pull together under pressure, sometimes even under the pressure of faulty leadership.

The members of the field team still regarded Sam's decision as a fool's errand. But rather than disobey him, in a split second they made a conscious decision to submit to the leader's authority for two simple reasons:

1. They had elected Sam to his post. Win or lose, as mature individuals they felt they would have to stand by the consequences of that decision.
2. They realized that if they openly resisted Sam's leadership simply because they didn't agree with his decision, they would be threatening the principle of teamwork, which they regarded as inviolate. What, their rational faculties asked them, was to stop someone else from doing the same thing to them when they were leading the team?

In that moment Bill, Kwame, and Bowie came together under their leader, even though they strongly suspected that he was leading them to defeat. They reached a decision to sacrifice the short win for the long-term win: upholding the team's integrity.

That was a mature decision, and a decision to be applauded because it was tacitly made by committee, as on any cohesive team. Within the space of a few minutes, I had watched a team on the brink of implosion pull itself together in the living embodiment of the principle that "if one of us fails, we all fail." Sam, they knew, had failed. But in the end they had succeeded by supporting him.

With winning teams, the burdens are shared, as are the rewards. Teams can achieve goals beyond the capacities of even the most talented individuals. No one scales Mt. Everest alone. No one wins a battle alone. No one builds a building alone. The real reason that winning teams win is that they are greater than the sum of their parts.

EIGHT

The Good Company

To: Carolyn Kepcher [E-mail]

I have been intrigued by your role on *The Apprentice* as "Donald Trump's right-hand woman" and am curious about what advice you might give to a second-year business student actively in search of a company that will bring out the best in him. Through my education I have learned about how to analyze business cases. But I have few ideas about how to pick a great company. If you have any ideas, suggestions or advice on solving this problem (and if you have the time!) your thoughts would be much appreciated.

Living Legacies

Whenever I have a few free moments at work (which isn't often), I try to take a walk around our golf course. It's a beautiful place. Walking around it clears my head. No single aspect of my ten years of experience on the property has been more exciting than being able to participate in its transformation from a neglected ugly duckling into a swan.

At a certain point in all our lives, we begin to think about leaving legacies. I know Donald Trump thinks about it. I know I think about it—and I'm just thirty-five! What we know inside The Trump Organization is that Donald Trump's legacy, as well as our legacy as a group, will be not just the properties we've constructed (or reconstructed)—the golf courses, hotels, apartment complexes, office complexes, casinos, and resorts—but the company and good name that our founder has built. For many visionary companies, and many visionary founders of companies, the true legacy lies in the daily fulfillment of goals that define a purpose and mission extending far beyond the lifetime of the founder.

To my correspondent MM, and to all my other readers and correspondents out there who ask me—frequently—what to look for in a company to join, my answer is twofold:

- A company that has been—or better yet, *is being*—built to last.
- A company that will bring out the best in you, where *you* will last.

The Company Woman

Let's face it: I'm a company woman. And you know, I'm proud of it. That term has taken on so many negative connotations, but it is possible today to be a company woman or man and not feel like some throwback to the fifties. "Company man" is an anachronistic phrase, harking back to a time that now feels like the Stone Age, when most people—almost exclusively men, often right out of high school or college—joined companies that were built to last. More often than not, those young people remained at those companies until they retired at sixty-five, which in those days felt *old*, far older than it feels today.

If you remained for your entire working life at the same company, your tenure there might be nearly fifty years. That's more than half the average lifetime! When you reached your mid-sixties, the company would typically throw you a big party and present you with a gold watch. That watch was, in effect, your fiftieth-anniversary present from the company.

The model of the paternalistic, long-term company was based on a tightly woven cluster of assumptions that, along with the phrase "company man," have unraveled in the ensuing decades:

- The company you joined would last for at least your lifetime, if not for centuries. At the end of your multi-decade stint at the company, you would receive not only the proverbial gold watch but a secure, comfortable, company-sponsored pension, intended only to be supplemented by personal savings and Social Security benefits.

- What you gave to the company, they gave back, all along and at the end.
- If you worked hard and kept your nose clean, you could be confident that you would climb steadily up the corporate ladder.
- The husband worked at the company and the wife stayed at home.

What a difference a few decades make! How many companies today can claim to offer lifelong employment security, a substantial pension, a secure climb up the corporate ladder, a salary sufficient to permit only one member of the husband-and-wife team to work outside the home? Decades of downsizing, reengineering, and tough foreign competition have left too many once-great organizations hollowed out and dispirited places where employees are often openly distressed that the unspoken contract that once defined their lives seems to have been not just broken but discarded, trampled upon, and burned.

When a company doesn't give its employees the sense that it cares about them, how can they care about the company? Think how many companies in recent years have sent their employees the chilly message "You're on your own. We'll let you stick around here for just as long as we can use you—or use you up!—and then we'll spit you out like a squeezed lemon."

I know I'm at a place where I want to stick around to collect my gold watch, and I couldn't be prouder of my identity as a company woman. The Trump Organization is at bottom an entrepreneurial company, still run by Donald Trump with a distinctive, surprisingly personal touch. And though Mr. Trump may not, for example, know the name of every employee in the organization, deliberately decentralized as it is, he knows a good many of them. We are often surprised by what he knows and what he remembers about everything we do—large and small. And what The Trump Organization has given us, its employees, is precisely what the most talented, ambitious people in business are interested in these days. More than money, more than stock options, more than our name on the door, or an impressive title that ultimately rings hollow, we want to gain and retain control of our own destinies. We want to be intrepreneurs, entrepreneurs within companies.

Since the new wave of employees, whether Gen X, Gen Y, or Gen Z, is not selfless, we want to share more fairly in the fruits of our labor than our parents did. If the company gets rich, we would like to get rich too, thank you very much. But it's not all about money, it's also about satisfaction and gratification. Though today we have images of employees shifting among companies at dizzying rates, the truth is a little more complex. If a company can provide its employees with the challenge of tackling the new, they will stay. If not, they will leave. So the new unwritten contract between the best companies and the best employees reads approximately as follows: If you give us the benefit of your creativity, your enterprise, your insights, we will provide you with compensations that include both money and challenge, growth, and the ability to be part of something bigger.

And at all the best companies, management has something priceless to offer: An opportunity to see to it that the projects you manage come to fruition.

So what, in today's fast-changing world, makes a good company?

GOOD COMPANY RULE 1:
A good company is a place where people are
deeply invested in accomplishing and completing long-term,
as opposed to short-term, goals.

The Gospel of Growth

Most for-profit companies, as we all know, tend to fixate on growth. By which they tend to mean exclusively financial growth: Annual revenue growth. Profit growth. Market share growth. Growth in stock price. Growth in brand value. Growth in just about any aspect of success you can measure. But what can't be measured (at least not yet) is that companies grow along these measurable dimensions only *when* and *if* they permit their employees to grow along with them.

Want my advice on finding a good company?

GOOD COMPANY RULE 2:
A good company knows how to hold on to its best employees
by giving them room to grow.

Here are some signs of such companies that can be easily obtained from a job interview or even the corporate website or promotional and recruitment materials:

- Employee retention that is longer by an average of five years than the industry standard
- A promotional track that includes frequent evaluation and landmarks for identifying and supporting the most able employees
- Educational reimbursement programs

Much as my experience staying with the same company has been positive, I know there are others who have not had my good fortune. For some, there are drawbacks to sticking with certain companies for a protracted period of time. The following is an example of why sticking around a company that doesn't permit its employees to grow can make one dread going to work.

A friend of mine has been at the same company for nearly eight years and recently shared with me her mounting frustration that, even as she has been promoted, senior management simply won't let her grow. They still see her as a junior executive, even though she handles her own accounts, and they treat other incoming hires with the same title and level of experience with higher esteem. Whether it is big, small, profitable, or unprofitable, a company that is not quick to recognize the abilities of its best, most loyal people will quickly lose those people. My friend has given her notice.

Brand Aid

People may say what they want about Martha Stewart or Donald Trump, but you have to hand it to both of them: they have created strong brands based on their outsize personalities. Both their companies, within a remarkably short time, grew to substantial presences in their industries for a simple reason: *They enjoyed strong, personal, and lasting bonds with their customers.* All the great brands, and all the visionary founders of great brands—Richard Branson of Virgin, Phil Knight of Nike, Henry Luce of Time-Life, Henry Ford of Ford, Donald Trump of Trump—have learned one lesson well in their lives:

GOOD COMPANY RULE 3:
A good company knows what its customers want.

A good company anticipates what its customers want, need, or aspire to sometimes before they know it themselves. I've seen it happen time and again in our organization, and it lies at the core of our creativity.

To be Trump now is to have a number of identifiable traits. In fact, they are so identifiable that I won't even bother to list them. Some people might dismiss these traits as mostly about surface glitz, but that is missing the point. To be Trump is to know what every Trump customer, in every industry or undertaking, wants without reservation: the best.

GOOD COMPANY RULE 4:
*A good company is one that has created a brand
known for being the best.*

Finding Your Challenges

A decade ago, I turned up at Briar Hall Country Club and was immediately intrigued by its distressed situation. I sensed an opportunity for a turnaround, and what drew me to the place was the idea of participating in that turnaround. I understood that I might have to wait a long time to be there when it finally happened. Through thick and thin—that is, a permitting process that turned out to be more arduous than any of us anticipated, ups and down in the residential real estate market, two terrible bosses, and other challenges along the way—I would have to see it through. But do you know what? To look at Trump National today with Briar Hall as my reference point only makes it that much more impressive to me.

How do any of us grow? How do we learn? Through experience. And I think we all can agree that soft experiences don't teach you nearly as much as hard experiences. When President John Kennedy pledged our country to send a man to the moon, he said we should shoulder this burden "not because it is easy, but because it is hard."

Every time I play or walk the courses at Trump National,

Bedminster, Trump International in Florida, and the other courses in our group, I am reminded that golf courses are designed to be difficult for a good reason. In golf as in life, Donald Trump and golfers like him enjoy facing obstacles and traps because they enjoy overcoming them. Difficult courses are *fun* for those who know how to play. And they make the win that much sweeter. The same goes for ski slopes, white water for rafters, mountains for climbers, and the settings of just about every recreational activity ever invented.

CAROLYN 101:
Succeeding at difficult tasks is what will make you great.

If you want my advice, when seeking a great company to join, don't look for the easy way out. Look for a company that will pose obstacles and challenges. Look for situations that will take you outside your comfort zone, test your spirit, and build up your strength. Top-flight organizations bring out the best in people—aspects, skills, talents, and traits they never even knew they had. Keep in mind that what you are doing today should be building the muscles and honing the skills that will allow you to take on those more challenging tasks tomorrow.

The great thing about great companies is that they don't let anyone sit idle for a moment, even if at times you may be wishing for a way to coast for a while. Through either strong motivation from a boss or powerful competition from within the team, high-performance organizations push you forward with a force that most people find impossible to resist.

When I first set foot on this piece of land a decade ago, I spotted a challenge. I sensed a risk and identified that risk as an opportunity for growth. I knew that the only direction we could go was up. And when I was given the backing of a great company to make it so, I realized there wasn't anything I couldn't achieve.

Delivering on Your Promise

From the moment he met me, Donald Trump got the idea that I was good at operations. That's why today I am not only an EVP (executive vice president) but also a COO (chief operating officer). I have a knack for making the trains run on time, for keeping close tabs on details, for making sure that what needs to get done gets done. So, like a good corporate executive, he hired me to work largely from my core competency: I became a senior operating officer who over time has assumed greater operational responsibilities, all in the same basic area: golf resort management. Instead of running one golf club, I now run several, and I will likely be running more in the future, as we are becoming a major force in a fast-growing industry.

And though my hands are clearly full there, I'm now what you might call a celebrity, if you will permit me to make the term a trifle elastic, thanks to *The Apprentice*. From a small speaking role, I have become somewhat of an icon or spokesperson for women in business, and I am proud to know that I am seen as a positive role model.

This is why I wanted to share my story—to show you how it could be done, just as I promised at the beginning of this book. I deliver on my promises. And now you need to deliver on your promise. Will you necessarily get a raise, a promotion, a better job, a bonus, or even a pat on the back from your boss from reading this book? Not if you don't go out and make it happen.

As you know by now, when I am faced with any new situation, my first question always is, "What are my resources?" My goal here has been to give you some of the resources you need to take on the tasks and challenges that lie ahead if you hope to achieve success in your career.

As for me, I am often asked where I intend to go from here. The short answer is that, with the backing of a great boss and a highly regarded company that allows me to be challenged, I can count myself fortunate not to have to go anywhere.

Acknowledgments

A debt of gratitude and innumerable thanks go to the following people, whose assistance, support, and friendship, at work and in life, have given me the reasons and the resources to fill the pages of this book.

To Esther Newberg, my literary agent at ICM, with whom I clicked right away, for recognizing this project's potential and facilitating its movement forward. Amanda Patten, my editor at Simon & Schuster, with whom it was a pleasure to work, for your vision and assistance in translating my ideas and advice into text. Steve Fenichell, my writer, for working with me—under such a tight deadline—to transform my story and thoughts into a book that sustains the delicate balance between business lessons and anecdotal humor. It was wonderful working with such a talented professional.

Donald Trump, this book is a giant-sized thank-you note to you for believing in me since day one, and for being the outstanding boss, mentor, and friend that you have been to me every day of the decade that has passed since we first met. Thank you!

George Ross, my partner on *The Apprentice*. Spending hours and days at a time agreeing and disagreeing with you during shooting is a joy . . . and by the way, executing a golf tournament is more difficult than planning a concert!

To the exceptional "downtown team" at The Trump Organization: Norma Foerderer, my friend and mentor; Allen Weisselberg; Bernie Diamond; Jeff McConney; Eric Sacher; Matthew Calamari; and Jason Greenblatt. Thank you for your support and for being one of my best resources and a smart, dedicated, great group of people. To the ladies: Robin Himmler, Rhona Graff-Riccio, and Meredith McIver, who do so much behind the scenes to keep The Trump Organization running.

Vinny Stellio and Tommy Fazio, for your creative talent and friendship. There are no two people with whom I would have rather built Trump National Golf Club in Briarcliff Manor, New York, and Bedminster, New Jersey.

Phillip Anastos, although you've moved on to bigger and better things, I am so thankful for your years of support, friendship, and professionalism.

One of the first lessons I learned was to surround myself with great people—in life and in business. I *have* these people: the department heads and staff at Trump National Golf Club in Briarcliff Manor, New York. Dan Scavino, my terrific assistant manager, thank you so much for your years of friendship. Cary Stephan, Peter Bell, Sandra Broas, Chris Devine, Blake Halderman, Tara Landau, Bill Keefe, Marie Siani, and David Bakyta—thank you for performing your jobs with the utmost professionalism and efficiency, and for making my job enjoyable while doing so. How lucky I am to work with such an exemplary team!

In his latest book Donald Trump writes, "Ask God for a great assistant . . . A great one can make your life a whole lot easier—or, in my case, almost manageable." Elizabeth Buchan, you are my godsend. You make my life not only manageable, but a pleasure as well.

Ashley Cooper, thank you for your friendship, your sense of humor, and your dedication in making Trump National Golf Club in Bedminster a success. And to the staff at Trump National Golf Club—Michael Fisher, Cory Fischer, Joe Isidori, Gloria Amos, and Greg Nicoll—thank you for your hard work and dedication.

The contestants of *The Apprentice*, it was wonderful stalking you and critiquing your every move! In getting to know you, I am confident that you are all destined for success. Bill Rancic, thank you for confirming that you are indeed the professional and gentleman I thought you to be.

Mark Burnett, you are one of the most amazing people I have ever met and I am lucky to be able to consider you a friend. The tremendous success of this show is a testament to your infinite creative genius.

Thanks to Jeff Zucker and his impressive, wonderful group at NBC, including Amanda Ruisi and Sean Martin. Jim Dowd, Senior Press Manager at NBC Entertainment Publicity, I have enjoyed working with you immensely. You are a true professional and friend.

To a truly creative and talented team at Mark Burnett Productions—executive producer Jay Bienstock; co-executive producer Conrad Riggs; supervising producer Kevin Harris; producers Katherine Walker, Jamie Bruce, William Pruitt,

James Canniffe, and Seth Cohen; the creative team of Rob LaPlante and Justin Hochberg; and a big thanks to Sadoux Kim, Jay Ostrowski, and Tom Borgnine—I have had such a blast working with all of you.

Raymond and Marie Cassidy—Dad and Mom—you were the loving leaders of the first team I was ever on. I could never thank you enough for all the lessons, guidance, love, and encouragement. I love you. My brother, Tom, and my sisters, Kathy and Linda, it was growing up with you three that made me so competitive. You are the best. I love you.

And finally, to my George. My rock, my shoulder to cry on, my partner in life. Thank you for being all those things and more. Thank you for all that you have done for our family, especially during the whirlwind that has been the past year and a half. I love you!

And my little darlings, Connor and Cassidy, just thinking about you makes me smile. You have brought so much happiness to my life.

ABOUT THE AUTHORS

CAROLYN KEPCHER is an Executive Vice President with the Trump Organization and the COO of Trump National Golf Clubs in New York and New Jersey. She has worked for The Trump Organization for nearly ten years and costars with her boss, Donald Trump, on the hit reality television series *The Apprentice*. She lives with her husband and two children in Ridgefield, Connecticut.

STEPHEN FENICHELL is the author of *Plastic: The Making of a Synthetic Century* and *Other People's Money*, as well as the coauthor of *Passport to Profits* with Mark Mobius and *A New Brand World* with Scott Bedbury.